Job Seeker's Faithful Guide

By Charles Caro

Dedication

For job seekers everywhere regardless whether they are unemployed, underemployed or simply seeking a better position. The job search journey can be very lonely and filled with frustration.

For my son, Mark, who strives every day to find peace somewhere between his ambitions and his limitations (p. 33).

Forward

There are many books written detailing the job search process covering everything from skills assessments and resume writing to interviewing and salary negotiations, but there is nothing available for the job seeker looking for something to sustain themselves mentally and spiritually. Being unable to sustain themselves mentally and spiritually many job seekers soon grow weary of the daunting job search journey and simply quit looking before they reach their goal.

The "Job Seeker's Faithful Guide" targets everybody involved in a career transition regardless whether they are unemployed, underemployed, seeking a new opportunity or launching a new business on their own. In fact, anyone in career transition is a job seeker.

One of the most difficult tasks a job seeker faces is how to sustain the mental and spiritual strength to make it through the complete journey. When a job seeker's mental and spiritual strength wanes the chances for success in the job search are drastically reduced, and finally the job seeker simply abandons the job search.

The "Job Seeker's Faithful Guide" provides a resource for anybody in career transition regardless of where they are along their job search journey.

How To Use This Book

The "Job Seeker's Faithful Guide" is organized as a series of sixty-six (66) "Reflections". The chapters are arranged in the order the individual "Reflections" were originally presented to members of the "In Between Jobs Support Group", which an outreach ministry of the St. Paul Roman Catholic Church located in Tampa, Florida.

The individual "Reflections" can be read and studied in any order without detracting from the value of the full content of the book. The book includes three (3) indexes at the end of the book as follows:

Topic Index - Lists job search related topics included in the book;

Scripture Index - Lists all scripture references included in the book;

Secular Reference Index - Lists all secular references mentioned in the book.

Each "Reflection" in the book includes a scripture reference followed by an updated application of the scriptural message using secular references, and finally a specific connection between the scripture and secular references as applied to the job search journey. Finally, "Reflections" include a set of self-discovery questions and a prayer.

Contents

Are You Wiping The Dust From Your Feet?

In the Gospel of Luke we are told the Lord appointed seventy others and sent them two and two ahead of him to every city and place where He Himself was going to come. His instructions were clear and precise regarding what each of the seventy must do when they came to a place where they were received, and He also gave instructions on what to do when they came to a place where they were not received.

> But whatever town you enter, and they do not receive you - go out into its streets and say. Even the dust from your town that cleaves to us we shake off against you; yet know this, that the kingdom of God is at hand. (Luke 10:10-11)

At first read it might be easy to think the Lord is telling the seventy to admonish those that don't receive them, but the words are used to provide a means for the seventy to carry on with their mission without the extra burden of the dust of their failures.

Everybody fails at one thing or another. It is impossible to go through life without failure, but what we do as a response to failure provides us with either an extra burden to carry or something to remind us that the kingdom of God is just that much closer.

In the job search process it is important for the job seeker to always remember to dust off their feet to be clear of the failures they encounter until they complete the mission of finding the new position God already knows is in their future.

1. Can you think of a time when you didn't wipe the "dust from your feet"?
2. How many ways in a job search should the job seeker remember to wipe the "dust from their feet"?

3. How can the job seeker turn the act of wiping the "dust from their feet" into a positive for their job search?

Prayer
Lord, I know you are trying to make clear to me that a life of faith is one of priorities, and ultimately one of grace. Help me better understand that I haven't "earned" my worth in life because of my credentials, or because of what I feel I have accomplished. My worth is a free gift, given from you, Oh might God. Please accept all those things I feel that I have accomplished, all the ways I have tried to please you Oh God by following your law blamelessly, and trusting in your Wisdom and promise. In Jesus name we pray Amen.

Who's Your Neighbor?

In the parable of the Good Samaritan (Luke 10:25-37) Jesus extends the obligations of the faithful toward each other to include those outside the community. By choosing as the hero of the parable a "Samaritan", Jesus makes him a doubly dubious character. First, as a "Samaritan", he is outside the "neighborhood" not only by location but also for being wholly outside the familial circle of traditional Judaism. Second, and more subtly, this "Samaritan" traveler is obviously wealthy. He is traveling with means. He has supplies, a ride, and cash-on-hand. In addition, he knows where to stay and who to contact. In other words, he is what people today would classify as "well connected". The "Samaritan" is the hero of the story because nothing motivates him other than his compassion. One of the least recognized things about the parable of the "Good Samaritan" is how important the use of labels is in the parable. In the parable of the "Good Samaritan" the robbed victim is the only one in the story without a label. We have a "Priest", a "Levite", a "Samaritan", an "innkeeper", and, of course, "robbers". Even an animal is labeled as a "beast". But, the person in danger is only identified as a "man". No label.

So the answer to the question of "Who's your neighbor?" is "Everyone is your neighbor." In a world where everyone and everything (cars, clothes, wine - you name it) has a label, Jesus turns over the label-makers' tables and gives this answer to the lawyer's question of "Who's your neighbor?". Your neighbor is every man. Your neighbor is every woman. Your neighbor is everyone.

When you come right down to it, all labels are meaningless, and not just for the one being labeled, but for the labeler as well. Jesus debunks the use of labels, which is why He doesn't label the three who came by as the three passersby, as he does in the three debtors' parable.

But at the core of the parable of the "Good Samaritan" is not a lesson about who is your neighbor (the lawyer's question). It is about how to "be" a neighbor. Jesus' answer to His lawyer interrogator is the same both times. Do. Act. For love is the ultimate verb.

A job seeker will first identify with the robbed man in danger, but Jesus would have even the job seeker think beyond the labels and recognize it is their role to also be the "Good Samaritan" and remember their neighbor is everyone.

1. Who do you most identify with in the parable of the "Good Samaritan"?
2. How many ways can you be a "Good Samaritan" for other job seekers?
3. Are you well enough connected, as the "Samaritan", to ensure you can be a good neighbor?

Prayer
Lord, give me the long view of my work and mission in this world. Help me to see that it is better to fail in a cause that will ultimately succeed Than to succeed in a cause that will ultimately fail. Inspire me to use all the talents you have gifted me with. Make me fair and honest in my dealings. Keep me away from personal worries that I may be able to give myself wholly to the challenges of my profession. Stop me for a minute of prayer to offer You everything I do. Amen.

Choosing The Better Part

The Lazarus siblings, Martha and Mary appear several times in the Gospel of Luke and John. The first encounter, which is detailed in Luke 10:38-42, is when Jesus comes to the home of Martha and Mary for supper. Martha welcomes Jesus into her home and soon becomes distracted by her many tasks in the kitchen. In the meantime Mary sat at the Lord's feet and listened to what Jesus was saying. Discouraged that she has been left to do all of the work Martha comes out of the kitchen and asks Jesus, "Lord, do you not care that my sister has left me to do all the work by myself? Tell her then to help me." But the Lord answered her, "Martha, Martha, you are worried and distracted by many things; there is need of only one thing. Mary has chosen the better part, which will not be taken away from her."

What bothers many reading the story of Mary and Martha is the implication the Lord approves of those turning their noses up at kitchen duty. Can it be this is the same Lord who urges us to be servants for all people?

Of course, there would be no story and no lesson without Martha's complaint. If Martha had remained quiet, Jesus would not have rebuked her. But, Martha complained, and Jesus supported her sister. The thing about the story not well understood today is by encouraging Mary to stay and listen to His teachings Jesus did a very important thing for women. During the time of Christ Jewish society did normally allow women to study Scriptures or even listen to the teachings of a rabbi.

The message of the story is multidimensional. At one level we learn the problem of making things more complicated than they need to be while also learning the value of spiritual food. On another level we learn it is more important to listen and learn before we act in haste creating more complications than results. On yet another level we see how Martha, who is a woman of action, is changed by the presence of the Lord.

But, what does the story of Mary and Martha have to do with being in the middle of a job search? Quite simply we learn the value of learning and listening before we devote too much time toiling at often unproductive tasks producing little or no results. We also learn that in showing devotion to the Lord our faith can bring unexpected and productive results.

Remember, Martha's older brother was Lazarus. Both Martha and Mary were heartbroken when Lazarus died, but it was Martha who went out to meet Jesus when she heard He was coming. It was Martha who said to Jesus, "If you had been here, my brother would not have died. But I know that even now God will give you whatever you ask" (John 11:21-22). And after the raising of Lazarus there is another dinner in Martha's home, but this time there is no complaint from Martha. Through it all we often overlook the most important thing the Gospels tell us about Martha. She opened her home to Jesus (Luke 10:38), and the Greek word for this literally means Martha received him under her roof. Zacchaeus (Luke 19:6) was the only other person mentioned in the New Testament for offering such warm hospitality.

"Behold, I stand at the door and knock," says Jesus. "If any one hears my voice and opens the door, I will come in to him and eat with him, and he with me" (Revelation 3:20).

As job seekers, we too can open our homes and hearts to Jesus. And if we do, he will teach us, correct us, and give us the opportunity for loving service.

1. How are our actions in a job search all too often more like the actions of Martha in the Kitchen?
2. Do we, as job seekers, spend too much time in action producing no results when we should spend more time listening to the teachings of those capable of showing a more productive path?

3. What can you do to better prepare yourself to open the door to a new and better way of approaching the job search?

Prayer
God give me faith in myself. Not only on the days when I am going great and winning and nothing seems impossible, but on days when I wonder if I am brave enough, smart enough, strong enough. Don't let me quit, not ever. Let me keep faith in myself. No matter how many people discourage me, doubt me, laugh at me, warn me, think me a fool, don't let me listen. Let me hear another voice telling me, "You can do it, and you will!" If nobody else in the whole world seems to care or believe in me, let me believe in myself. I know there will be times when I doubt my own ability, I will be discouraged, on the verge of despair. Don't let me give up, hang on to me. Fan the fires of my faith so that I will try even harder. Give me even more faith in myself. You are the source of my abilities and my faith. I know that you will give me what I ask . . . Faith in myself through your power and glory. Amen.

On Forgiveness And Encouragement

In Damascus there was a disciple named Ananias. The
Lord called to him in a vision, "Ananias!" "Yes, Lord,"
he answered. The Lord told him, "Go to the house of
Judas on Straight Street and ask for a man from Tarsus
named Saul, for he is praying. In a vision he has seen a
man named Ananias come and place his hands on him
to restore his sight." "Lord," Ananias answered, "I
have heard many reports about this man and all the
harm he has done to your saints in Jerusalem. And he
has come here with authority from the chief priests to
arrest all who call on your name."
(Acts 9:10-14.)

Ananias' first reaction regarding what the Lord was asking
him to do is one of dismay because clearly Saul (Paul) had been
identified as an enemy to all of the Lord's followers. When the
Lord insisted that Saul would be His "chosen instrument"
Ananias did as he was told.

To forgive someone for a hurt they have caused is not an
easy thing to do, but holding hatred and bitterness towards
others will ultimately destroy us. We can literally feel the pain
caused by hatred and bitterness through a mounting sense of
the stress we experience, and the stressors in life can have a
major impact on our physical, mental, and spiritual health.
Such stressors can cause us to strike out at others, including
those we love the most, and, in turn, our stressors get
replicated in the heart and mind of those we contact. The
weight of the world may crush in against us, and still we may
refuse to give up our grievances.

The solution offered by the Lord is truly radical. For the
Lord there is no question of revenge or even bare restitution.
His message is that we become the shock absorbers of this
world:

"But I tell you who hear me: Love your enemies, do good to those who hate you, bless those who curse you, pray for those who mistreat you. If someone strikes you on one cheek turn to him the other also. If someone takes your cloak, do not stop him from taking your tunic. Give to everyone who asks you, and if anyone takes what belongs to you, do not demand it back. Do to other as you would hve them do to you." (Luke 6:27-31)

Ananias was obedient to his vision, but even so Saul (Paul) did not meet with such ready acceptance from his fellow Christians. It wasn't until Barnabas, who was nicknamed "Son of Encouragement" by the apostles, took Saul (Paul) to the apostles did they accept him as a true brother in Christ.

The way Barnabas championed Saul (Paul) as a new convert was echoed a few years later when Paul himself had a falling out with a young disciple named John Mark. For reasons we will never know John Mark had left to go home halfway through his first missionary journey with Paul and Barnabas. In planning a second journey Barnabas wanted to take John Mark again, but Paul absolutely refused feeling someone who had let them down once would surely do the same a second time. As a result, the two evangelists parted company with Barnabas and John Mark going one direction while Paul went off in an entirely different direction with his new companion, Silas.

The willingness of Barnabas to give John Mark a second chance was soon justified. Just a few years later writing from his prison in Rome to the church at Colosse, Paul sent greetings from Mark, who had been a "comfort" to him. More significantly, this same Mark is thought to have been the author of St. Mark's gospel.

1. How difficult is it for us to grant forgiveness while not forgetting how much we have needed forgiveness?

2. How does the difficulty in granting forgiveness to past employers hamper our current job search?
3. How can you see and feel the stressors in our lives impacting those we hold most dear?

Prayer

Lord sometimes I just want to give up. My burdens are overwhelming. I don't seem to ever catch up. I can't seem to get started. I feel the pain of stress, hurt and setbacks. Strengthen me to stand up knowing you are always with me. Fall fresh on me today so I can find my joy and peace again. Restore the broken places in my life. I need this pressure of stress to decrease. I want to have the resources and love required to provide for me and for my family. I desire the energy and motivation to perform my job and daily tasks at home. Amen.

Let's Talk About Accomplishments

Many of the most familiar parts of the Bible detail accomplishments. Indeed, most of how folks define and describe major personalities in the Bible come from descriptions of their specific deeds and accomplishments. Detail regarding specific accomplishments becomes the core message. Here are some examples taken from different parts of the Bible.

In the beginning God created the heavens and the earth. The earth was without form and void, and darkness was upon the face of the deep; and the Spirit of God was moving over the face of the waters. And God said, "Let there be light:; and there was light. And God saw that the light was good; and God separated the light from the darkness. God called the light Day, and the darkness he called Night. And there was evening and there was morning, one (Genesis 1:1-5)

Make yourself an ark of gopherwood; make rooms in the ark, and cover it inside and outside with pitch. And this is how you shall make it: The length of the ark shall be three hundred cubits, its width fifty cubits, and its height thirty cubits. You shall make a window for the ark and you shall finish it to a cubit from above; and set the door of the ark in its side. You shall make it with lower, second, and third decks. And behold, I Myself am bringing floodwaters on the earth, to destroy from under heaven all flesh in which is the breath of life; everything that is on the earth shall die. But I will establish My covenant with you; and you shall go into the ark – you, your sons, your wife, and your sons' wives with you. And of every living thing of all flesh you shall bring two of every sort into the ark, to keep them alive with you; they shall be male and female. Of the birds after their kind of animals after their kind, and of every creeping thing of the earth after its kind, two of every kind will come to you to keep them alive. And

you shall take for yourself of all food for you and for them. Thus Noah did; according to all that God commanded him, so he did.
(Genesis 6:14-22)

Now both Jesus and His disciples were invited to the wedding. And when they ran out of wine, the mother of Jesus said to Him, "They have no wine." Jesus said to her, "Woman what does your concern have to do with Me? My hour has not yet come". His mother said to the servants, "Whatever He says to you do it." Now there were set there six waterpots of stone, according to the manner of purification of the Jews, containing twenty or thirty gallons apiece. Jesus said to them, "Fill the waterpots with water." And they filled them up to the brim. And He said to them, "Draw some out now, and take it to the master of the feast." And they took it. When the mast of the feast had tasted the water that was made wine, and did not know where it came from (but the servants who had drawn the water knew), the master of the feast called the bridegroom. And he said to him, "Every man at the beginning sets out the good wine, and when the guests have well drunk, then the inferior. You have kept the good wine until now." This beginning of signs Jesus did in Cana of Galilee, and manifested His glory; and His disciples believed in Him. (John 2:2-11)

When the day was now far spent. His disciples came to Him and said, "This is a deserted place, and already the hour is late. Send them away, that they may go into the surrounding country and villages and buy themselves bread; for they have nothing to eat." But He answered and said to them. "You give them something to eat." And they said to Him, "Shall we go and buy two hundred denarii worth of bread and give them something to eat?" But He said to them, "How many loaves do you have? Go and see." And when they found out they said "Five, and two fish." Then He

commanded them to make them all sit down in groups on the green grass. So they sat down in ranks, in hundreds and in fifties. And when He had taken the five loaves and the two fish, He looked up to heaven, blessed and broke the loaves, and gave them to His disciples to set before them; and the two fish He divided among them all. So they all ate and were filled. And they took up twelve baskets full of fragments and of the fish. Now those who had eaten the loaves were about five thousand men.
(Mark 6:35-44)

Accomplishments are used to truly make the Word jump off the page, but there are many more things described in the Bible much less exciting or immediately memorable. The Bible includes things like "begets", rules, location descriptions, along with other detail as part of the full content of the Bible. Folks return to the Bible again and again because of the accomplishments, and each time someone returns to the Bible they wind up learning much more than they might have imagined.

The same is true when job seekers use memorable accomplishments when presenting themselves during a job search. Once a job seeker gains the attention of an employer with the details of their accomplishments they gain the opportunity to tell the employer more about themselves and in doing so they gain the opportunity to present a better case for getting hired.

1. What are your favorite accomplishments from the Bible?
2. Do detailed quantified accomplishments jump out of your resume?
3. What can you do to make your accomplishments truly grab the attention of potential employers?

Prayer

Lord, guide me in my attempts to let others know of my accomplishments and give me the strength to continually present my case through action knowing my actions will always speak louder than just my words. Amen.

Amazing Grace

And when there had been much dispute, Peter rose up and said to them: "Men and brethren, you know that a good while ago God chose among us, that by my mouth the Gentiles should hear the word of the gospel and believe. So God, who knows the heart, acknowledged them by giving them the Holy Spirit, just as He did to us, and made no distinction between us and them, purifying their hearts by faith. Now therefore, why do you test God by putting a yoke on the neck of the disciples which neither our fathers nor we were able to bear? But we believe that through the grace of the Lord Jesus Christ we shall be saved in the same manner as they." (Acts 15:7-11)

In the passage above Peter declares in a very diplomatic manner the core nature of grace virtually wherever it is referenced in the Bible and throughout theological writings. The grace given by the Lord is not given because we have necessarily earned the grace or even because we might feel we deserve the grace, but rather because the grace is for Him to give regardless of what the recipients have done or deserve.

Indeed, the principle and most basic prerequisite for receiving grace, which is frequently referenced as an "undeserved blessing", is for the recipient simply to be present to receive the grace. For some simply being present seems like too much effort while they may claim they are just as much "deserving" of receiving grace as those putting forth the effort to be present. What those not putting forth the effort even to be present forget is the test of being "deserving" is truly not part of the equation for determining who is to receive the grace.

In many ways a job is similar to grace, not only because almost everybody sees a job like grace as a blessing but also because at the very core of the seeming similarities is the hard cold truth in the fact a job is not something a person should never see as something they truly deserve.

More so than at any time in the past getting a job and holding a job requires being present on a day-in-day-out basis. Getting a job requires every bit as much energy and effort as keeping a job, and those not willing to be present at all times during the job search may find it increasingly difficult to ever get to the place where they actually have a job.

It may come as a surprise to hear an unemployment rate of 5 to 5½% is considered full employment, and full employment is usually equated with natural unemployment, which is the amount of unemployment consistent with an expanding, growing economy that has no inflation. Of course, even full employment does not consider literally millions of people not even looking for work.

So, but for the grace of God those either holding a job or seeking a job would be amongst those totally out of the job market.

1. What part do you think being present for a job search equates to being present to receive grace?
2. As with grace, are you doing all you can to be present in your job search?
3. What do you do or what can you do at times when you feel yourself slipping from being present?

Prayer
May the grace of our Lord Jesus Christ, and the love of God, and the fellowship of the Holy Spirit be with us all, now and evermore. Amen.

With God's Help

Have you ever heard or read something sounding very biblical and wondered whether or not the source was the Bible? For example, "Work like it all depends on you and pray like it all depends on God." sounds very biblical, but the exact wording can be found nowhere in the Bible. Perhaps the closest phrasing for the words is an oft quoted passage found in Matthew.

> Then He said to them, "My soul is exceedingly sorrowful, even to death. Stay here and watch with me." He went a little further and fell on His face, and prayed, saying, "O My Father, if it is possible, let this cup pass from Me; nevertheless, "not as I will, but as You will." Then He came to the disciples and found them sleeping, and said to Peter, "What? Could you not watch with Me one hour". "Watch and pray, lest you enter into temptation. The spirit indeed is willing, but the flesh is weak." (Matthew 26:38-41)

From "watch and pray" we get the message to "work like it all depends on you and pray like it all depends on God". Both messages seem simple enough, but both omit stating the difficulty facing not only the disciples but also anybody else trying to apply the message to actual day-to-day practice. Indeed, the spirit is willing, but the flesh is weak.

It takes true strength of purpose to stay the course and apply the message to the tasks at hand. To compound the message even further we need to consider more closely the meaning of "with God's help". We all know God has a plan, but our free will certainly has an impact on the course of our journey. What we do also impacts the path for many others our life may touch along the journey.

Indeed, we might reasonably find God's help is delivered through the hands and deeds of others just as we, too, may be called to be the conduit for delivering help to someone else.

Striking the balance between doing nothing, which illustrates the "flesh is weak" course, acting purely in our self-interest, and acting in our "best interest" is always difficult, and the notion our "watch" obligation extends to others serves to complicate our range of choices on a daily basis.

God's help does come for us all, and sometimes we have to recognize we become the delivery conduit from God's help to others. Operating in life on the basis of working solely to help ourselves while also expecting God's help diminishes our role in the way God's help reaches us all.

1. What temptations distract you for doing all you can with your job search?
2. Do you remember to heed a calling to help others with their job search?
3. What more could you do to ensure God's help reaches us all?

Prayer

God give me faith in myself. Not only on the days when I am going great and winning and nothing seems impossible, but on days when I wonder if I am brave enough, smart enough, strong enough. Don't let me quit, not ever. Let me keep faith in myself. No matter how many people discourage me, doubt me, laugh at me, warn me, think me a fool, don't let me listen. Let me hear another voice telling me, "You can do it, and you will!" If nobody else in the whole world seems to care or believe in me, let me believe in myself. I know there will be times when I doubt my own ability, I will be discouraged, on the verge of despair. Don't let me give up, hang on to me. Fan the fires of my faith so that I will try even harder. Give me even more faith in myself. You are the source of my abilities and my faith. I know that you will give me what I ask . . . Faith in myself through your power and glory. Amen

How To Be Your Own Evangelist

Anybody involved in a job search should be prepared to announce good news related to their experience and ability to be a good employee. The word "evangelist" is derived from a Greek word meaning "to announce good news". Somewhere along the line the meaning of "evangelist" has taken on a meaning more identified with a tent revival than "announcing the good news", which is why most folks start getting squeamish when anybody even mentions they should be more like an evangelist in their job search. Getting back to the root meaning of the word "evangelist" should make it much easier to take in the notion of becoming more of an evangelist in the job search process.

As with the early disciples, anybody involved in a job search must be willing to step out of their "comfort zone". It wasn't easy for the disciples, and at first it won't be easy for the job seeker.

As with the early disciples, all job seekers must be prepared with knowledge of the good news they wish to spread, which means all job seekers must know not only their skills but also how to put their skills to good use during the job search. Being armed with a complete understanding of their own good news gives any job seeker a head start on the road to a new opportunity.

Georgia O'Keeffe, who was an American artist beginning her career as a serious artist in 1916 at a time when women weren't expected to have any career outside the home, became known as the "Mother of American Modernism". There is a quote attributed to Georgia O'Keefee providing rich insight for the job seeker. The quote is as follows:

"Where I was born and where and how I have lived is unimportant. It is what I have done with where I have been that should be of interest".

Getting to the point where Georgia O'Keeffe's words truly make sense for the job seeker defines what it takes for the job seeker to be truly effective at the task of being their own evangelist and announcing their own good news.

Assertiveness applied to announcing the good news ignites the job search process not only for the individual job seeker but also for anybody encountering the job seeker along the way.

Richard Nelson Bolles presents some excellent recommendations for an assertive approach to the job search in his book titled "What Color Is Your Parachute". The recommendations include the following:

Plan your job search with a clear goal in mind: decide what you want to do, where you want to do in, and for whom.

Claim the highest level of skill you legitimately can: you are more likely to find a job and the job can be more uniquely tailored to you.

Find and meet the employer you want to work for: show the person who has the power to hire you just how you can help fill the needs of that organization.

1. Have you defined what you have as good news?
2. What do you need to be more comfortable outside your comfort zone?
3. Have you had trouble defining what you have done with where you have been?

Prayer

Our Father, we thank you for all the opportunities we have from day-to-day for learning, for fun, and for fellowship. Bless, we pray, that each day may broaden our horizons a bit further than the day before, that we may always praise you with spirit and with understanding. Amen.

Be Mindful Of Your Be-Atitudes

Whether we know it or not every minute of every day we present ourselves to the world revealing not only what we openly choose to show to the world but also many of the things we might hope were hidden from view. Such is the nature of how our "attitude" intersects with how closely we come to following the teachings known as the "beatitudes".

For someone engaged in a job search the intersection of "attitude" and "beatitudes" is something to be mindful of throughout the day with every task undertaken during the day regardless of whether or not the task is directly related to the job search because even tasks seemingly unrelated to the job search process have an impact on how the job seeker conducts themselves while directly engaged in a job seeker task.

Whether we like it or not we can never get too far from the realities of life and how each part of our life gets wrapped up along with the whole sum of our life experiences and daily interactions. In a very real sense the words of William Shakespear from "As You Like It" are very true.

"All the world's a stage, And all the men and women merely Players; They have their Exits and their Entrances, And one man in his time plays many parts."

While there is a grain of truth in Shakespear's words with each of us playing the role in some extended improvisational theater play titled "This Is Your Life" where each response from another actor can send the whole play careening off in some new and totally unexpected direction. Being in a job search is one of those sudden reversals. At such times we can get more caught up in the melodrama of our lives and forget the "world's our stage" where we can choose the course we wish to take because one of God's gifts to us all is free will.

Using our free will we each can choose to make the course correction necessary being mindful of the teachings found in the "beatitudes". In the "beatitudes" we learn what the Lord intends for us to do in the course of our interactions with others in our own personal space on the world's stage.

The New Testament provides two renditions of the "beatitudes". The renditions come from the Gospel of Matthew and the Gospel of Luke. The separate renditions have many common points, but the "beatitudes" from the Gospel of Luke do more to inform us all regarding the turns in life and how we should continue along our path at times of trouble and sudden reversals of fortune. How we exercise our use of free will play a very important part in the course of our journey across the world's stage and beyond.

1. Is your attitude getting in the way of your ability to follow the path defined by the "beatitudes"?
2. If the world is a stage, are you getting too wrapped up in turning your life into a melodrama when you should be focusing more on exercising you free will to get off in a direction of your choice?
3. What helps you on a day-by-day basis to stay grounded in the "beatitudes" rather than being caught up in a play not of your choosing?

Prayer
Lord, enlighten me to journey only and always in charity and with my gaze fixed on heaven, my ultimate destination. Lord, be my guide, so that I may have complete self-control, a sure eye, and constant moderation. Lord, be for me everywhere, and for those whom I accompany or meet along the way. Amen.

With A Mustard Seed And The Branches

> Then He said, "to what shall we liken the kingdom of God? Or with what parable shall we picture it? It is like a mustard seed which, when it is sown on the ground, is smaller than all the seeds on earth; but when it is sown, it grows up and becomes greater than all herbs, and shoots out large branches, so that the birds of the air may nest under its shade. (Mark 5:30-32)

> I am the vine, you are the branches. He who abides in Me, and I in him, bears much fruit; for without Me you can do nothing. If anyone does not abide in Me, he is cast out as a branch and is withered; and they gather them and throw them into the fire, and they are burned. If you abide in Me, and My words abide in you, you will ask what you desire and it shall be done for you. (John 15:5-7)

In parable and discourse the Lord prepares His disciples for the journey and mission ahead of them. Indeed, their journey and mission is to build the kingdom of God by spreading the Word of the Lord. The parable of the mustard seed is very important for the disciples to hear. The Lord knows none of his disciples are world leaders, great statesmen or great generals, but they have been called to literally change the world. The Lord knows each of the disciples will wonder during the darkest of nights whether or not they have made a mistake. So, the Lord gives them a parable letting them know they will succeed because from the smallest of seeds the Word will grow to start a mighty tree.

What difference could one small mustard seed make in the world? Remember, every person that has ever trusted Jesus as Savior can trace his/her spiritual roots back to one of the one of the eleven disciples hearing the Lord's first telling of the parable of the mustard seed.

As job seekers and those who would be part of the support team for other job seekers, we go forth with a similar journey and mission knowing we too carry a mustard seed in the form of the preparations done to ensure the seed is properly sown.

From the discourse found in John 15:5-7 we are told we all come from the one true vine and no matter where our journey and mission leads we can never be far from the one true vine.

As job seekers, we hold true to the belief the Lord is with us throughout the journey knowing there is a plan and His will be done.

1. When the nights are long and dark what reminds you of the mustard seed parable?
2. Do you fully understand the value of the mustard seed parable being important for job seekers?
3. What reminds you on a day-by-day basis of the presence of the Lord in your life?

Prayer
God, thank you for the mustard seed although it is so small. God, thank you for the plant that grows up largest of them all. God, thank you for the birds that sing in branches that reach wide. God, thank you for the words you teach while walking by my side. God, give us love and strength to meet each other's human need. God, bury me to rise again just like the mustard seed. Amen.

Say A Little Prayer

Both the Old Testament and New Testament of the Bible include hundreds of prayers, and many of those prayers we hear on a very regular basis. Most of the prayers are found in parts of the Bible familiar to all, but hidden in the least read section of one of the least read books of the Bible we find a real gem. The first nine chapters of 1 Chronicles list the begets for the family tree of the Hebrew tribes beginning with Adam and proceeding through thousands of years to Israel's return from captivity. Exactly the stuff someone would never want in their resume, but then in chapter 4 there is a sudden and unexpected break after forty-four names.

> Now Jabez was more honorable than his brothers, and
> his mother called his name Jabez, saying, Because I
> bore him in pain". (1 Chronicles 4:9)

The translation of the Hebrew word "Jabez" is pain. All babies arrive with a certain amount of pain, but Jabez's birth apparently went beyond the usual enough pain so his mother felt the need to memorialize the birth by naming of her new son Jabez.

Clearly there was something special about this man Jabez. It stopped the historian in mid-drone because the next verse is what has come to be known as the prayer of Jabez.

> Oh, that You would bless me indeed, and enlarge my
> territory, that Your hand would be with me, and that
> You would keep me from evil. (1 Chronicles 4:10)

In the next verse the list of begets continues with the tribe of Judah as if nothing had happened, but the one sentence prayer certainly seems to have changed the life of Jabez.

The prayer of Jabez begins simply enough by asking for a blessing, which is something many of us forget to ask every time we pray. Consider for a moment the blessings we might have received had we only asked for the blessing.

> Ask, and it will be given to you; seek, and you will find; knock, and it will be opened for you. For everyone who asks receives and to him who knocks it will be opened. (Matthew 7:7-8)

Each of us is limited in what we think of as our territory, especially in a job search because we think in terms of "My abilities + experience + training + my personality and appearance + my past + the expectations of others = my assigned territory" when God's math the terms would be "my willingness and weakness + God's will and supernatural power = my expanding territory".

1. When was the last time God worked through you in a way it left you with no doubt of His work?
2. Why not ask?
3. How does God's math work for you in your job search?

Prayer
Oh, that You would bless me indeed, and enlarge my territory, that Your hand would be with me, and that You would keep me from evil, that I may not cause pain! Amen.

Hope - A Call-To-Action

Hope is much more than just a state-of-mind which promotes a positive outcome for events and circumstances in our life. Hope is more than the feeling about what is wanted can be had or how events will turn out for the best or even the act of looking forward to something with desire and reasonable confidence.

Charles Snyder, Ph.D., who was one of the first developers of positive psychology, created his "hope theory" while on sabbatical from the University of Kansas. Through his observations of people and his interactions with them Snyder was able to build his own definition of "hope". For Snyder "hope is the sum of the mental willpower and waypower that you have for your goals". Snyder's expanded definition of "hope" blends in three (3) underlying concepts:

Goals: "Goals are objects, experiences, or outcomes that we imagine and desire in our minds". Snyder ranks goals involving hope to fall somewhere between impossibility and a sure thing;

Willpower: "Willpower is the driving force in hopeful thinking". An individual's willpower depends on how well they understand their goal. Based on collected tacit knowledge psychotherapy techniques are used to zoom in on a person's desires and wishes, on how they focus on their goals, and their ability to obtain or attain their goals.

Waypower: "Waypower reflects the mental plans or road maps that guide hopeful thought". It is the waypower providing an individual with the ability to plan through to a goal and to map out a plan. Snyder says hope is the "mental willpower and waypower for goals".

As a part of Snyder's work he developed what he labeled a **"Hope Scale"**, which measures a person's intended succession in congruence to their goals. Overall, an individual's determination to achieve their goal is their measured hope.

In Romans 8:24-25 the Apostle Paul states "For we were saved in this hope, but hope that is seen is not hope; for why does one still hope for what he sees? But if we hope for what we do not see, we eagerly wait for it with perseverance", which fairly closely follows what Snyder has defined as "hope".

So, like "success" is a "journey" rather than a "destination" the nature of "hope" is the combination of "vision" forged with "willpower" and ultimately tempered with "waypower" directed to an achievable goal.

Albert Einstein said, "Learn from yesterday, live for today, hope for tomorrow". However, for best results the job seeker should heed the words of David Orr when he said, "Hope is a verb with its shirtsleeves rolled up."

1. What is the difference between hope and optimism?
2. Do you need the most help with "Goals", "Willpower" or "Waypower"?
3. Where do you see yourself on a "Hope Scale"?
4. Are your shirtsleeves rolled up?

Prayer
You know my dreams, Lord, and I know it is a lot to ask to realize those dreams, but I ask that you hear my prayer of hope. I would like to think that my hopes and dreams are all part of your plans for me, but I trust that you always know better. I put my dreams in your hands to mold and fit to your will. I surrender my hopes to you. Amen.

The Power Of Words

"In the beginning was the Word, and the Word was with God, and the Word was God." (John 1:1)

Words have special meaning in virtually all folks do day-in and day-out. Certain words and phrases convey a message transcending print and speech.

For example, mention "John 3:16" to almost anybody and they will know what you are referencing even though they may not be able to quote the verse verbatim.

"For God so loved the world that He gave His only begotten Son, that whoever believes in Him should not perish but have eternal life." (John 3:16)

Some words and phrases become iconic virtually from the time they first appear.

When any American or someone with even a passing exposure to American History sees or hears "Four score and seven years ago" they automatically think of Abraham Lincoln and the U.S. Civil War. In just ten sentences President Lincoln was able to summarize his view of the war.

When anybody sees or hears "That's one small step for man, one giant leap for mankind." they immediately think of Neil Armstrong and him stepping to the surface of the Moon.

As a job seeker, the words used in networking, a resume, and interviews don't have to be so iconic, but the words used are still very important. The words a job seeker uses will almost always make the difference between being successful with the job search and not being successful with the job search.

In the current job search climate the importance of a job seeker's words is more important than ever. There have been times when it might have seemed simply showing up was all it took to get hired. Indeed, at the end of the 1990s someone could have what amounted to a one sentence resume, especially when the words they used included the following:

COBOL maintenance programmer with ten (10) years major corporate experience.

Such words on a resume were absolutely golden, and such a person could virtually name their rate. Today it takes much more to attract and hold the interest of potential employers.

The goal of every job seeker should be to have the power of words necessary to present themselves in a manner capable of moving them from the role of job seeker to role of being fully employed.

1. How much do you struggle to get the right words in front of potential employers?
2. Does your networking, resume, and interview skills match your objectives and talent?
3. Are the words you use in your networking, resume, and interviews working with you?
4. What do you need to be better prepared to use the power of words in your job search?

Prayer

Father, keep before us the wisdom and love you have revealed in your Son. Help us to be like him in word and deed. We ask this through our Lord Jesus Christ, your Son, who lives and reigns with you and the Holy Spirit, one God, for ever and ever. Amen.

Hold Your Ground

The Kansas state motto is "Ad Astra Per Aspera", which is Latin for "To the stars through difficulties". The motto refers not only to the pioneering spirit found in early settlers but also the difficult times Kansas went through prior to becoming a state. In times of trial and tribulation it is important to remember the importance of holding your ground because failing to do so changes the person or people in ways beyond recovery.

In many ways the job search process has a lot in common with the life of an early settler in Kansas or even one of the early apostles. At some point along the path of a job search the job seeker will feel as Paul in Timothy.

> "At my first defense no one stood with me, but all forsook me. May it no be charged against them. But the Lord stood with me and strengthened me, so that the message might be preached fully through me, and that all the Gentiles might hear. Also I was delivered out of the mouth of the lion. And the Lord will deliver me from every evil work and preserve me for His heavenly kingdom. To Him be glory forever and ever. Amen! (2 Timothy 4:16-28)

Sometimes the job seeker is sure to feel like the civil engineer mumbling to himself, "When you are hip deep in alligators it is difficult to remember your job is to drain the swamp".

For the job seeker the call "Hold your ground" means more than simply holding on to what has been previously achieved but also holding on to the idea of being a person of value and principle. The real challenge is being able to hold the ground and not get caught up in allowing pride to undercut the realities of the situation. At the end of the job search the job seeker should be able to sense having held the ground on values and principle while also winning the battle with pride.

1. What does "hold your ground" mean in your job search?
2. When does the job search process most stress your feeling about being able to hold your ground?
3. When the challenge of the job search process pushes you to the limit what helps you get back on track?
4. Has the challenge of "holding your ground" caused you to change or reconsider your course along the way in the job search process?

Prayer
Thank you for not only understanding our hardships and heartaches, but for embracing them and experiencing them as your own, as one of us. And, thank you that you endured through it all, and considered such a life well worth living. Lord, this is hard! Lord, we are so easily discouraged, so easily distracted, so easily dismayed, so easily entangled. Show us that our problems aren't any greater or worse than those of others. Lift our eyes up to see you and follow you in running the race and running it well. For the sake of Jesus, who endured to the end. Amen.

What Color Is Your Teahouse?

Every job seeker has heard of Richard Bolles' book titled "What Color Is Your Parachute". The book is billed as a practical manual for job hunters and career changers. It is a playbook for job seekers wanting to get ahead of the pack with their job search. Using the book should really help any job seeker just as having the assistance of a career coach should help with the job search. Of course, like any plan, which is a tool, there is always a way to get off track. If the job seeker doesn't put the energy and effort necessary into using the tools available to them, things can get off the line quickly.

In 1956 MGM released a delightful movie illustrating how the very best of intentions can get sidetracked. The title of the movie is "Teahouse of the August Moon" with Marlon Brando (Sakini), Glenn Ford (Captain Fisby), Paul Ford (Colonel Purdy), and Machiko Kyo (Lotus Blossom). The movie is set in 1946 on Okinawa during the Occupation of Japan. Sakini, who is an Okinawan interpreter, opens the film with a brief history of Okinawa and concludes his narration by saying, "Pain makes man think. Thought makes man wise. Wisdom makes life endurable". The story is about how US Occupation Forces were used to teach the Japanese about democracy.

Colonel Purdy assigns Captain Fisby to Tobiki. Fisby's guide for doing his job is titled "Plan B", which details his mission, including the construction of a schoolhouse in the shape of a pentagon. After appointing village leaders Fisby decides the villagers can produce souvenirs for sale in base exchanges. Many complications follow. All of the women in the village want what Lotus Blossom has, and Fisby's solution is to let Lotus Blossom give the village women lessons on how to be geishas. All of the village men want a teahouse, so material for the schoolhouse goes into building a teahouse.

When the village men return from trying to sell their souvenirs with no sales all seems lost. Fisby tries to console the villagers, but Sakini says it's OK we will just go home and get drunk. Fisby says that would be nice, but there is nothing to drink. Sakini quickly corrects Fisby by saying they have home brewed sweet potato brandy.

Suddenly Fisby realizes Tobiki has a product in high demand throughout occupied Okinawa and beyond. They find a fancy translation for sweet potato and brand their product as "Batata Brandy". One outbound call produces an unending stream of orders for 7 star Batata Brandy, which takes seven days to produce. Thus, the Tobiki Brewing Cooperative is born.

During the celebration of the completion of the teahouse Purdy arrives and discovers not only there is no schoolhouse but also the brewing business, which he thinks is immoral. Purdy also thinks the cooperative is Communism. Purdy orders the destruction of all the stills and brandy plus the dismantling of the teahouse.

After everything is apparently, destroyed Purdy gets a message about a Congressman coming to Tobiki to see the great success in Tobiki. Purdy is desperate, but Sakini reveals he has only made in seem like all was destroyed, but, in fact, everything of value was only hidden. All is saved. One of the last things Fisby says to Sakini is "I have found peace somewhere between my ambitions and my limitations."

For the job seeker the story illustrates the need to clearly identify their skills and ambitions along with their limitations to ensure a result producing peace for all.

1. Have you been completely honest with yourself and those coaching you regarding your skills?
2. During your job search have you been focusing your thoughts to make you wise?
3. Who is the Colonel Purdy in your job search?

Prayer

All through this day, Blessed Lord, please guide us safely and surely wherever we go, whatever we do. Help us to reach our goals. We ask this not only for ourselves, but for all job seekers. We want You close beside us today and always. Amen.

Water In The Desert

A long time ago and in a land far and away thousands of refugees from Egypt are moving relentlessly towards what they have been told is the "Promised Land", but they are hungry, thirsty and feeling they are lost in the desert. Though troubled the refugees reaffirmed their faith and believed their efforts in the desert would bring them to the "Promised Land."

"Our fathers ate the manna in the desert; as it is written. 'He gave them bread from heaven to eat." (John 3:31)

More then a millennia later there is a man sitting beside a well wearied by his journey across the desert. The man is Jesus. Soon a woman of Samaria comes to the well to draw water. Jesus says to her "Give me a drink". The woman of Samaria asks Jesus, "How is it that You, being a Jew, ask a drink from me a Samaritan woman?"

Jesus answered and said to her, "If you knew the gift of God, and who it is who says to you, 'Give Me a drink', you would have asked Him, and He would have given you living water" The woman said to Him, "Sir, You have nothing to draw with, and the well is deep. Where then do You get that living water? Are you than our father Jacob, who gave us the well, and drank from it himself, as well as his sons and his livestock? Jesus answered and said to her, "Whoever drinks of this water will thirst again, but whoever drinks of the water that I shall give him will never thirst. But the water that I shall give him will become in him a fountain of water springing up into everlasting life." (John 4:10-14)

The woman of Samaria with faith and belief asks Jesus to give her the living water.

Nearly two millennia later another man wearied from a journey across a desert in the southwestern United States comes across a marvelous sight in the form of a water pump. Upon closer inspection he finds a note stuffed inside a bakin' powder can.

"This pump is old", the note began, "but she works so give'er a try. I put a new sucker washer in 'er, you may find the leather dry. You've got to prime the pump, you must have faith and believe. You've got to give of yourself 'fore you're worthy to receive. Drink all the water you can hold, wash your face, cool your feet. Leave the bottle full for others, Thank You kindly, Desert Pete".

Of course, the man at the water pump is from the Kingston Trio song titled "Desert Pete".

Now millions of job seekers are moving through the desert between jobs and finding their thirst in need of quenching every bit as much as anybody in history. A closer look at the millions of job seekers reveals some are making much better progress through the desert than many others because they too have faith and believe while giving of themselves along the way.

1. Describe your quest for water in the desert during your job search?
2. What is keeping you from priming the pump with the resources available to you?
3. What barriers are preventing you from making the best of your job search?

Prayer
God of life, God of all those who walk miles for water in their desert, may water, clean and life-giving, be available to all in need. May that vision move forward. Amen.

Don't Ask Alice When Setting Goals

Everybody sets goals, but the process of setting goals leading to productive outcomes requires thought and careful consideration because mistakes in goal setting wastes time and usually leads to unexpected destinations.

In Philippians Paul the Apostle relates the following:

I press toward the goal for the prize of the upward call of God in Christ Jesus. Therefore let us, as many as are "mature", have this mind; and if in anything you think otherwise , God will reveal even this to you. Nevertheless, to the degree that we have already attained, let us walk by the same rule, let us be of the same mind. (Philippians 3:14-16)

How goals are set can take many forms. Each approach leads to more or less success. Even not setting goals leads to a destination, as Alice learned in Lewis Carroll's "Alice's Adventures In Wonderland."

"Cheshire Puss," she began, rather timidly, as she did not at all know whether it would like the name: however, it only grinned a little wider. "Come, it's pleased so far," thought Alice, and she went on. "Would you tell me, please, which way I ought to go from here?"

"That depends a good deal on where you want to go," said the Cat.

"I don't much care where —," said Alice.

"Then it doesn't matter which way you go," said the Cat.

"— so long as I get *somewhere*," Alice added as an explanation.

"Oh, you're sure to do that," said the Cat, "if you only walk long enough."

Job seekers have a choice of setting goals using George T. Doran's "SMART Goals" approach or they can use what could be called the "ALICE Goals" approach.

A "**SMART Goal**" must be "Specific", "Measurable", "Attainable", "Relevant", and "Time-bound".

A "**ALICE Goal**" must be "Arbitrary", "Limitless", "Impossible", "Capricious", and "Enigmatic".

Regardless of how the job seeker opts to set goals they, as the Cheshire Cat confirms, are sure to get to a destination, but using the "SMART Goal" approach is sure to produce much better results than the "ALICE Goal" approach.

1. What do you think of the "ALICE Goal" approach?
2. Has your goal setting approach been more like the "SMART Goal" or "ALICE Goal" approach?
3. What can you do when your goal setting approach is mostly like the "ALICE Goal" approach?
4. What needs to happen before you are ready to set more "SMART Goals" than "ALICE Goals"?
5. Would switching from "ALICE Goal" setting to "SMART Goal" setting be your first "SMART Goal"?

Prayer

Lord, Thank you for the gift of this day. Thank you for the inspiration you give us to dream and to set goals for ourselves. We realize we are not guaranteed tomorrow, let alone the rest of today. But setting goals gives us the motivation to live out each day purposefully and with direction. So I pray that you would help us all set meaningful goals and then equip us to fulfill them. We submit each and every goal to you. May our goals reflect your will for our lives and may they glorify you. We pray for others who have goals and dreams that they desire to see happen. May you also equip them to reach those precious desires. Fill us with your awesome purpose in Jesus name Amen.

Skills On The Table

Perhaps the most fundamental task in any successful job search is for the job seeker to identify, detail, highlight and apply their skills. Once the job seeker gets a firm grasp on what they can do it becomes much easier to not only describe accomplishments but also make the connection between their skill set and what their future employer needs to see in the form of value when evaluating all potential candidates.

"As each one has received a gift, minister it to one another, as good stewards of the manifold grace of God." (1 Peter 4:10)

Whether a person is Apostle, Bishop, Priest, Deacon, or a member of the laity they all have received gifts in the form of skills enabling them to minister to one another. These gifts from God are an integral part of the makeup of every individual. Each individual becomes the steward of their gift in the form of skills, and with the manifold grace of God each individual applies their skills even in ways they might not have ever imagined.

In 1998 Harrison Ford and Anne Heche starred in a movie titled "Six Days Seven Nights". Harrison Ford is "Quinn Harris", who is a former airline pilot now running his own one plane charter service. Anne Heche is "Robin Monroe", who is a journalist at a major fashion magazine. Robin and her boyfriend are on a South Seas island holiday, and Quinn is the pilot for the final leg of their travel. The first morning on the island Robin is asked by her boss to fly back to Tahiti to do an interview. She charters Quinn's plane for the flight back to Tahiti. During the flight Quinn and Robin are caught in a massive thunderstorm, blown way off course, and crash land on a deserted island beach at night. The morning after the crash Robin and Quinn discuss their situation.

Robin: Aren't you one of those guys?
Quinn: What guys?

Robin: Those guy guys, you know, those guys
with skills.
Quinn: Skills?
Robin: Yeah. You send them into the
wilderness with a pocket knife and a
Q-tip and they build you a shopping
mall. You can't do that?

Quinn seriously underestimated his skills because over the next few days he prepares a peacock supper, converts the damaged DeHavilland Beaver to be a flight worthy seaplane, defeats a band of Maori pirates, and gets the two of them back to civilization. Clearly Quinn's skills, by the manifold grace of God, were enough to save the day.

All too often job seekers seriously underestimate their skills, and far too many job seekers never take the time to fully catalog their skills. Job seekers forget it probably cost their employer 100-200% of their salary to find a replacement or even retain the value they had added to the organization. Job seekers should never leave their skills on the table, and by the manifold grace of God take the time to be good stewards of what has been given to them.

1. Have you underestimated the extent and value of your skill set?
2. Have you truly done a good skills assessment for yourself?
3. What skills add the most value for your job search?
4. Can you match your skills with opportunities meeting between your ambitions and limitations?

Prayer

Lord, be with me today in identifying my skills and finding employment. Lead me to work that I love, and that has value. Guide me to a place with an atmosphere of respect and cooperation, in a safe and happy environment. Help me to find fulfillment mentally and financially. Amen.

The MacGyver Approach To Interviewing

Interviewing skills are key to a successful job search because the interview step of a job search puts the job seeker and potential employer in direct realtime contact.

In each of the Synoptic Gospels we see Jesus being interviewed by the Pharisees. In each telling from the Synoptic Gospels it is clear Jesus was not only well prepared to face the Pharisees but also he was able to use things he didn't even bring with him to support his presentation. None illustrates the preparedness of Jesus better than the following:

Then the Pharisees went and plotted how they might entangle Him in His talk. And they sent to Him their disciples with the Herodians, saying "Teacher, we know that You are true, and teach the way of god in truth; nor do You care about anyone, for You do not regard the person of men. Tell us, therefore, what do You think? Is it lawful to pay taxes to Caesar, or not?" But Jesus perceived their wickedness, and said, "Why do you test Me, you hypocrites? Show Me the tax money." So they brought Him a denarius. And He said to them, "Whose image and inscription is this?" They said to Him. "Caesar's". And He said to them, "Render therefore the things that are Caesars's, and to God the things that are God's." (Matthew 22:15-21)

The notion of being not only prepared for any situation but also, if anything, over prepared for any situation presented itself on a weekly basis from 1985 to 1992 in each new episode of "MacGyver". No matter what came his way MacGyver was always able to work out a solution for whatever was facing him, his mission or those he was trying to protect. MacGyver explained what he was doing best in the pilot episode during an exchange with Andy Colson, who was Chief Operations Officer for a classified underground laboratory facility.

Colson: You know it's going to take a lot more than you can carry in that knapsack to get you through all of this.

MacGyver: Well, the bag is not for what I take Colson. It is for what I find along the way.

With cause job seekers fret over the interviewing process, and sometimes the fretting gets in the way of doing well during the interview. Doing something in realtime with no do-overs is stressful, especially when a lot rides on the outcome. The job seeker should be prepared not only for what they think might happen in the interview but also for virtually anything possible in the interview, which means they must carry with them the virtual equivalent of MacGyver's knapsack.

1. Do you spend more time preparing answers for stock interview questions than on how to handle and answer scenario questions directly related to the company and position?
2. How do you go about researching a company before an interview?
3. Have you thought about how you will handle information you learn only at the interview?
4. What would you most like to put in your interview knapsack during the interview process?

Prayer
Lord, Help me to give of my best in all of my interviews. Wrap me in your loving arms when I feel insecure. Hold me in your steady embrace when I feel nervous. Help me to understand the questions I am asked, And answer in a honest and inspired way. I pray you would show me if this is the right job for me. I am your servant and I seek to do your will on this earth. Lead me in your paths and guide me into all truth. In His name we pray. Amen!

Getting The Lint Out During Lent

According to the Catholic Encyclopedia, "the real aim of Lent is, above all else, to prepare men for the celebration of the death and Resurrection of Christ . . . the better the preparation the more effective the celebration will be. One can effectively relive the mystery only with purified mind and heart. The purpose of Lent is to provide that purification by weaning men from sin and selfishness through self-denial and prayer, by creating in them the desire to do God's will and to make His kingdom come by making it come first of all in their hearts."

At its roots Lent is a journey of conversion, turning more completely to Christ and His way of life. The journey during Lent must always involve giving up sin in some form, which is where the notion of giving up something for Lent originates. The goal is not simply abstain from sin during Lent but to root sin out forever. Thus, in the context of Lent the "Conversion" means leaving behind an old way of living and acting in order to embrace a new life in Christ.

The purification accompanying the journey through Lent involves internal housekeeping. For the job seeker getting rid of what doesn't work moves the job seeker closer to God's plan. What doesn't work can include getting rid of bad habits, thoughts, perceptions, and practices holding the job seeker back from the opportunity He has already put in the job seeker's path. By moving forward with the "Conversion" integral to Lent the job seeker moves closer to God and His plan.

Therefore purge out the old leaven, that you may be a new lump, since you truly are unleavened. For indeed Christ, our Passover, was sacrificed for us. Therefore let us keep the feast, not with old leaven, nor with the leaven of malice and wickedness, but with the unleavened bread of sincerity and truth.
(1 Corinthians 5:7-8)

Is this not the fast that I have chosen: To loose the bonds of wickedness, To undo the heavy burdens, To let the oppressed go free, and that you break every yoke. (Isaiah 58:6)

Lent is the time to once again make the "Conversion" to Christ and His way of life, but for the job seeker Lent is also a time to once again cast off bad habits related to the job search and renew a commitment to following the job search path leading most directly to career opportunity at the end of the journey. The purification and "Conversion" available to the job seeker during Lent provides a way to get all of the lint in the form of bad habits out of the job seeker's way to ensure a clear path along the job search journey.

1. Can you see the purification process of getting rid of bad job seeker habits as a way of preparing for the celebration of the death and Resurrection of Christ?
2. What would you define as a bad job seeker habit?
3. What bad job seeker habit would you most like to get rid of during Lent?
4. How can you work with others to be more successful in getting rid of bad job seeker habits?

Prayer
Almighty God, to you all hearts are open, all desires known, and from you no secrets are hid; Cleanse the thoughts of our hearts by the inspiration of your Holy Spirit, that we may perfectly love you and worthily magnify your holy name, through Jesus Christ our Lord. Amen.

The Benefits Of Helping Others

There are many places in the Bible where the benefits of helping others are seen to be not only good deeds but also a means of showing faith and being worthy of receiving help. Here are but a few such instances:

But do not forget to do good and to share, for with such sacrifice God is well pleased. (Hebrews 13:16)

Let each of you look out not only for his own interests, but also for the interests of others. (Philippians 2:4)

Give, and it will be given to you: good measure, pressed down, shaken together, and running over will be put into your bosom. For with the same measure that you use, it will be measured back to you. (Luke 6:38)

What does it profit, my brethren, if someone says he has faith but does not have works? Can faith save him? If a brother or sister is naked and destitute of daily food, and one of you says to them, "Depart in peace, be warmed and filled." but you do not give them the things which are needed for the body, what does it profit? Thus also faith by itself, if it does not have works, is dead. But someone will say, "You have faith, and I have works." Show me your faith without your works, and I will show you my faith by my works. (James 2:14-17)

The cover story of the March 1, 2014 issue of CIO titled "Dark Days of the Unemployed CIO" was written by Kim S. Nash, who is also the Managing Editor of CIO. The article chronicles the experience of several CIOs suddenly finding themselves in the job market, but none stands out more the story of Mark Stone, who found himself thrown into the job market in February 2009 when Zale simply did away with his CIO position. The last time Mark had a current resume was 14 years in the past, and he hadn't thought to build his peer network over the years. Stone floundered with his attempts to use his Rolodex for leads, and when he did nab a meeting he couldn't explain what he did best. "I was ill-prepared for interviewing. The job market had changed." he says, "I was clueless." At the edge of an abyss Stone, who holds a BBA in Accounting and was then a recently earned Master of Divinity, launched himself on a new vision of networking based on what he viewed as an "economy of goodwill". His goal was to help as many people as he could with mentoring, job tips, and technology advice. At breakfasts, lunches, professional groups and conferences he spread his "pay-it-forward" attitude. Along the way he honed his pitch and uncovered a treasure chest of companies and opportunities hidden only from those not willing to look. In six months he landed a CIO position with Safety-Kleen, which is an environmental clean-up company. In January 2013 after three years he once again found himself without a job, but because he had kept himself engaged in his network he soon received lots of leads. "They've now got the opportunity to help me back," he says, "It was lighting a match to a pile of kindling". In April 2013 he accepted the CIO position at Texas A&M University Systems. Stone's most sincere advice to job seekers is, "Never ever disappear."

1. In your life where is the balance between serving your interests and the interests of others?
2. How much of Mark Stone's story about the job search journey matches your job search story?
3. How can you focus your job search by using the lens of an "economy of goodwill"?

Prayer

We thank You for the many gifts You give us throughout our lifelong journey of faith. With hope, we ask You to nourish us in Your Spirit so we may be faithful stewards of Your gifts. With love, may the sacrifice of our giving be an outward sign of the true treasure we hold in Jesus. Keep us mindful of the good that can happen when we allow You to work through us united in faith. Amen!

You Can Never Have Too Many Skills

Throughout life everybody picks up new skills. Sometimes skills are learned without even knowing about it. Habits are a form of skill, and some habits just aren't productive. However, most of the skills a person really wants to acquire are learned as the result of three factors coming together to focus on the task of skill acquisition. Focused skill acquisition requires a goal, an opportunity, and the desire to see the task through to completion.

Proverbs from the Bible and cultures far from origins of the Bible provide an echo of what is required to go about focused skill acquisition.

Give instruction to a wise man, and he will be still wiser; Teach a just man, and he will increase in learning. (Proverbs 9:9)

Give a man a fish and you feed him for a day. Teach a man to fish and you feed him for a lifetime. (Chinese proverb)

In the 1950 movie titled "The Black Rose" the lead character is Walter of Gurnie (Tyrone Power), who is a Saxon Englishman of noble but clouded birth. He returns home from his studies at Oxford for the funeral of his Father where he learns his Father had acknowledged him in the his will, but only to the extent of naming him as a son and leaving him a pair of boots. When Walter of Gurnie speaks up for his Saxon heritage, his Father's Norman second wife accuses him of treason. The King (Michael Rennie), who walks in on the funeral while out hunting, intervenes and says it is a family matter. In the evening Walter of Gurnie returns to the castle with some friends to free some Saxon men detained in the castle. By the end of the evening both Walter of Gurnie and his bowman friend Tristram Griffin (Jack Hawkins) find no option other than to journey east to Cathay (China) in search of treasure and knowledge.

By the time Walter of Gurnie reaches Cathay he has learned many new skills, but he is still bitter about his life in England while Tristram Griffin continues to have great affection for the scent of England. Along the road to Cathay they have traveled with the warlord Bayan (Orson Wells) and wind up hiding Maryam (Cécile Aubry), who is an girl of English descent. Walter of Gurnie, Tristram Griffin and Maryam soon become the permanent "guests" of the dowager Empress of China where they learn even more new skills. When the trio learns they aren't really safe they devise a plan to escape using their skills, but only Walter of Gurnie and Maryam manage to escape safely albeit separately. Once Walter of Gurnie arrives back in England he is rewarded for the knowledge he brings back with him, and he is knighted. In the end Walter of Gurnie finds good use for the many skills he learned while traveling outside of England, and he also is reunited with Maryam thanks to Bayan's skills as a warlord.

A job seeker is on a journey outside of their comfort zone and they, too, must set a goal to learn new skills by taking advantage of the opportunity presented by extra time available during a job search. Their desire to complete the task of learning new skills is fueled by how they perceive those new skills might be applied in their new job.

1. What new skills do you need to enhance your ability to get hired in a new position?
2. Does the list of skills you would like to learn include a mix of people and technical skills?
3. Do find you have learned some bad habits preventing your from learning the skills you need?
4. What can you do to break bad habits while focusing more on developing good learning skills?

Prayer

Help us never to allow any habit to get such a grip of us we cannot break. Specially keep us from all habits which would injure our body or our mind. Help us always to do our best with your help to keep our body fit and healthy, and our mind clean and pure. Help us at present to discipline and train ourselves, to learn and to study, so that some day we may be able to do something worthwhile for the world and for You. This prayer we make for your love's sake. Amen.

Standout By Being True To Yourself

One of the best ways for a job seeker to get noticed is to be doing something more or different than everybody else, but in the process of trying to do something more or different the job seeker all too often forgets the best way to truly standout is to be true to them.

And you shall know the truth, and the truth shall make you free. (John 8:32)

For what profit is it to a man if he gains the whole world, and loses his own soul? Or what will a man give in exchange for his soul? (Matthew 16:26)

Nor shall you swear by your head, because you cannot make one hair white or black. But let your "Yes" be "Yes", and your "No," "No". For whatever is more than these is from the evil one. (Matthew 5:36-37)

And He said to me. "My grace is sufficient for you, for My strength is made perfect in weakness." Therefore most gladly I will rather boast in my infirmities, that the power of Christ may rest upon me. Therefore I take pleasure in infirmities, in reproaches, in needs, in persecutions, in distresses, for Christ's sake. For when I am weak then I am strong. (2 Corinthians 12:9-10)

What did Christ say to Pilate? "I came into the world to testify to the truth. Everyone on the side of the truth listens to me." (John 18:37).

"What is truth?" Pilate asked. Jesus didn't give a response to Pilate because in the context of the passage "truth" is not a noun to be parsed. Instead "truth" is a verb to be lived. By his actions Jesus showed the entire world the meaning of "truth" through his actions. By being true to His word He proved He was a man of character.

54

In 1988 Harrison Ford, Melanie Griffith, and Sigourney Weaver starred in a movie titled "Working Girl". Tess McGill (Melanie Griffith) earned her college degree with honors by attending night classes, but she is still trapped in a secretary position. When her boss Katherine Parker (Sigourney Weaver) breaks her leg skiing Tess takes advantage of the absence to advance her career by doing something to standout from the crowd. Tess teams up with Jack Trainer (Harrison Ford), who is an investment banker in need of a good deal, to present an acquisition deal to a major corporation. Of course, the situation gets complicated, but all works out by the end credits. Two quotes from the film illustrate how Tess managed to standout by being herself.

> Katherine Parker: Dress shabbily; they notice the dress. Dress impeccably; they notice the woman - Coco Chanel!

> Jack Trainer: You're the first woman I've seen at one of these things that dresses like a woman, not like a woman thinks a man would dress if he was a woman.
> Tess McGill: Thank you I guess.

1. What is "truth" in the context of standing out by being true to yourself?
2. Have you ever seen somebody standout by being themselves and succeed in the process?
3. How does standing out by being yourself help during the job search process?
4. What can you do to help you do a better job of standing out by being yourself?

Prayer

Lord, help us to always remember to be as You have created us. May each day bring us closer to becoming a living replica and example to others of how Christ lived here on earth and how You would want others to see Him through us. We give thanks for Your blessed guidance and divine protection not only for today but also for each day of our lives. In Jesus name, Amen.

Too Many Resumes?

In a job search a resume is the job seeker's equivalent of a business brochure. A resume presents the job seeker's experience, accomplishments, and education to potential employers in a format designed to bring job seeker and employer to the table for a face-to-face interview. Very few job seekers get to the interview without a resume, but at some point the job seeker really needs to ask whether or not they may have too many resumes.

When Christianity began its spread from the Holy Land the message presented by the disciples was clear and consistent. Even today with many different denominations the core message remains true to the Gospel and teachings of Jesus. The clear and consistent message delivered by all in the name of Jesus is very powerful, and the message comes from what amounts to one resume defining Christianity. Some examples of the importance of one clear and consistent message coming from the Bible include the following:

> For the word of god is living and powerful, and sharper than any two-edged sword, piercing even to the division of soul and spirit, and of joints and marrow, and is a discerner of the thoughts and intents of the heart. (Hebrews 4:12)

> I became a minister according to the stewardship from God which was given to me for you, to fulfill the word of God, the mystery which has been hidden from ages and from generations, but now has been revealed to His saints. (Colossians 1:25-26)

> There is one body and one Spirit, just as you were called in one hope of your calling; (Ephesians 4:4)

In 1992 Jack Palance won both an Oscar and a Golden Globe in the "Best Actor in a Supporting Role" category for his portrayal of an aging cowboy known only as "Curly" in the movie titled "City Slickers", which was released in 1991. Curly is the Trail Boss for dude ranch cattle drive experience targeted to middle aged big city men trying to work through a mid-life crisis. Curly teaches his would be cowboys many lessons, including some important lessons in life.

> Curly: Do you know what the secret of life is? [holds up one finger]
> Curly: This.
> Mitch: Your finger?
> Curly: One thing. Just one thing. You stick to that and the rest don't mean ...
> Mitch: But, what is the "one thing?"
> Curly: [smiles] That's what *you* have to find out.

By the way, when accepting his Oscar Jack Palance flopped down to the floor, did a series of one-handed pushups, stood up, spoke calmly for a while longer and even added a slightly risqué joke just to show everybody what an old guy can do when necessary.

1. How many resumes is "too many resumes"?
2. In thinking about your own resume(s) is there a clear and consistent message?
3. If someone truly has clear and concise goal for themselves, why do they need multiple resumes?
4. What can you do to reduce the number of resumes you need in your job search?

Prayer
Please help us find our purpose in life even though we have a feeling of being lost. To find a career which will enable us to do God's will, which will bring us joy and take away anxiety and despair. Please open the doors necessary for us to move forward in a positive light. Amen.

Job Seekers At The Fork In A Road

The second longest narrative in the Gospel of John is found in Chapter 11, which most people think is all about the resurrection of Lazarus of Bethany. The narrative from Chapter 11 includes many notable verses, including the following:

> "I am the resurrection and the life. He who believes in Me, though he may die he shall live. And whoever lives and believes in Me shall never die." (John 11:25-26)

The narrative includes the verse "Jesus wept" (John 11:35), which is famously cited as the shortest verse in the King James Version of the Bible, and it includes Jesus' cry to Lazarus once the stone is removed from the cave where Lazarus is entombed. Yet the main theme behind the narrative is not how Jesus resurrected Lazarus.

The main theme concerns what Jesus does at a very important fork in road along the way to Jerusalem and his own death and resurrection. By the time Jesus first hears the news of Lazarus being sick it is highly likely Lazarus was already dead because by the time Jesus finally arrives at the grave site Lazarus has been dead for four days. Apparently it was a one day walk from where Jesus received the news and the grave site, but what happens during the four days becomes a crucial part of Jesus' final journey to Jerusalem. The interval serves to provide Jesus with the time to do some teaching and get back to the basics of why his path must lead to Jerusalem for one very special Passover. Jesus knew the importance of the journey, and he also knew he could not fault anyone or anything around him for his situation. The return to basics during the four day interval provides the substance necessary to move the full story of His journey to its final destination.

By 1972 the son of an Italian immigrant born in St. Louis, Missouri with an eighth grade education became the greatest catcher in Major League Baseball history. As a player, coach, and manager he would appear in 21 World Series. As a player he would appear in 14 World Series with ten championships, both of which are records. He established World Series records for the most games (75), at-bats (259), hits (71), doubles (10), singles (49), games caught (63), and catcher putouts (457). For seven consecutive seasons from 1949 through 1955 he led the Yankees in RBI, and his teammates included stars like Mickey Mantle and Joe DiMaggio. In five seasons he had more home runs than strikeouts. For all of the superlatives related to his career in Major League Baseball more people remember Lawrence Peter "Yogi" Berra for his pithy comments and witticisms, known as "Yogiisms" than for any of his achievements in baseball. Three of Yogi Berra's most famous quotes apply to getting back to basics and taking the fork in the road.

If you come to a fork in the road, take it.

If you don't know where you are going, you might wind up someplace else.

I never blame myself when I'm not hitting. I just blame the bat and if it keeps up, I change bats. After all, if I know it isn't my fault that I'm not hitting, how can I get mad at myself?

Job seekers need to recognize reaching a fork in the road, get back to basics, and take stock of their situation while not blaming either equipment or their situation. Taking the fork with a new focus on the basics aids the job seeker immensely because without a focus on the basics they are sure to wind up someplace other than their intended destination.

1. Can a job seeker sense they have reached a fork in the road along their journey to a new job?
2. Who or what is the blame when a job seeker gets to a "hitting" slump?
3. What does getting the focus back to basics mean to you as a job seeker?

4. What can you do to stay focused on the basics during your job search?

Be A Part Of Your Own Support Team

One very important measure of an individual's success is in the nature and strength of the support team they have been able to assemble for themselves. The success of any support team is weakened when the support team doesn't fully include the individual. This is particularly true during the job search and other times of transition, especially when the individual also forgets about the constant level of support coming from and through the Lord. The measure of self-confidence or lack of self-confidence comes not just from within but also from faith.

References to self-confidence in the Bible always tie the measure of self-confidence with faith. For example:

Let us therefore come boldly to the throne of grace, that we may obtain mercy and find grace to help in time of need. (Hebrews: 4:16)

Therefore do not cast away your confidence, so that after you have done the will of God, you may receive the promise. (Hebrews 11:35-36)

I was with you in weakness, in fear, and in much trembling. And my speech and my preaching were not with persuasive words of human wisdom, but in demonstration of the Spirit and of power, that your faith should not be in the wisdom of men but in the power of God. (1 Corinthians 2:2-5)

Albert Frederick Arthur George was born in 1895, as the second son of Prince George Frederick Ernest Albert (Duke of York) and Princess Victoria Mary of Teck (Duchess of York). By his second birthday young Albert had become "His Royal Highness Prince Albert of York", but he was not expected to ever inherit the throne. As a young boy Prince Albert suffered from ill-health. In 1920 he was created Duke of York, Earl of Inverness and Baron Killarney, and he took on more royal duties. However, his stammer, his embarrassment and his tendency to shyness made him appear much less impressive than his older brother Edward.

In December 1936 history took a turn when Prince Albert's older brother, who had become King Edward VIII abdicated in order to marry his mistress, Wallis Simpson.

In 2010 a movie titled "The King's Speech" presents the story of how an unsure King George VI (Colin Firth) of the United Kingdom of Great Britain and Northern Ireland with the help of a speech therapist became truly worthy of his title. One of the key lines in the film defining his growth as King is as follows:

If I'm King, where's my power? Can I form a government? Can I levy a tax, declare a war? No! And yet I am the seat of all authority. Why? Because the nation believes that when I speak, I speak for them. But I can't speak.

In finding his voice King George VI found his self-confidence and became a part of his own support team just as each job seeker must find a way to become a part of their own support team.

1. Can a job seeker be a part of their own support team without being self-confident?
2. What hurdles does a job seeker face each day in maintaining their self-confidence?
3. Do you sometimes feel you are not part of your own support team?
4. What can you do to become more fully a member of your own support team?

Prayer

Lord Jesus Christ, You were poor And in distress, a captive and forsaken as I am. You know all man's troubles; You abide with me when all men fail me; You remember and seek me; It is Your will that I should know You And turn to You. Lord, I hear Your call and follow; Help me. Amen.

(Dietrich Bonhoeffer, Letters and Papers from Prison)

Are You Listening?

"Are you listening?" Hearing the question makes most people cringe, especially when the person asking the question is a spouse and your mind has been on something else. In fact, hearing and not understanding or hearing and not really listening happen frequently. Such situations happen more often than anyone would care to admit. The Bible is full of places where people were present and seemingly hearing, but nobody was truly listening.

The ear that hears the rebukes of life will abide among the wise. He who disdains instruction despises his own soul, but he who heeds rebuke gets understanding. The fear of the Lord is the instruction of wisdom, and before honor is humility. (Proverbs 15:31-33)

The heart of the prudent acquires knowledge, and the ear of the wise seeks knowledge. (Proverbs 18:5)

Therefore whoever hears these sayings of Mine, and does them, I will liken him to a wise man who built his house on the rock: and the rain descended, the floods came, and the winds blew and beat on that house; and it did not fall, for it was founded on the rock. (Matthew 7:24-25)

Therefore lay aside all filthiness and overflow of wickedness, and receive with meekness the implanted word, which is able to save your souls. But be doers of the word, and not hearers only, deceiving yourselves. For if anyone is a hearer of the word and not a doer, he is like a man observing his natural face in a mirror; for he observes himself, goes away, and immediately forgets what kind of man he was. But he who looks into the perfect law of liberty and continues in it, and is not a forgetful hearer but a doer of the work, this one will be blessed in what he does. (James 1:21-25)

In 1939 Dietrich Bonhoeffer's book titled "Life Together: The Classic Exploration of Faith in Community" was published, and the ministry of listening was a very key theme in the work. Here is an excerpt:

It is little wonder that we are no longer capable of the greatest service of listening that God has committed to us, that of hearing our brother's confession, if we refuse to give ear to our brother on lesser subjects. Secular education today is aware that often a person can be helped merely by having someone who will listen to him seriously, and upon this insight it has constructed its own soul therapy, which has attracted great numbers of people, including Christians. But Christians have forgotten that the ministry of listening has been committed to them by Him who is Himself the great listener and whose work they should share. We should listen with the ears of God that we may speak the Word of God.

The job seeker's task is doubly difficult because the job seeker must listen not only to those around them but also their own inner voice, and all the while the job seeker must listen for the word of God.

1. Have you caught yourself hearing something when you should be listening for something else?
2. Is the difference between hearing and listening a matter of what takes top priority at the time?
3. Do you listen as much as you hope others will listen to you?
4. What can you do to become a better listener and how will that help you in your job search?

Prayer

Lord we pray to be better listeners. Open our ears and cleanse our hearts so we all can share a true dialogue with each other rather than be inundated in a cacophony of monologues. Give us the ability to hear and receive Your word so we can attain wisdom and knowledge concerning Your will for us amongst our brothers and sisters each and every day. Amen.

A Time For Doing

Making time for "doing" has been a topic of interest since the very beginning of recorded history. Indeed, there would be no history unless many individuals and groups put time in to "doing" something. The most useful and inspirational mentions of work and "doing" in scripture are those where the "doing" and the "time for doing" is focused on something leading to a positive outcome. For example:

The man who plants and the man who waters have one purpose, and each will be rewarded according to his own labor. For we are God's fellow workers; you are God's field, God's building. (1 Corinthians 3:8-9)

Let your light shine before men in such a way that they may see your good works, and glorify your Father who is in heaven. (Matthew 5:16)

From the fruit of his mouth a man is satisfied with good, and the work of a man's hand comes back to him. (Proverbs 12:14)

The hand of the diligent will rule, while the slothful will be put to forced labor. (Proverbs 12:24)

There are certainly benefits in "doing", but creating the "time for doing" can difficult even in the best of times. Harvey MacKay, who is a businessman, author, and syndicated columnist, describes "time" as follows:

Time is free, but it's priceless. You can't own it, but you can use it. You can't keep it, but you can spend it. Once you've lost it you can never get it back.

In 1986 Ron Howard directed a film titled "Gung Ho". The film tells the story of how a dying car industry factory town in Pennsylvania brings a Japanese car company to town to reopen the town car factory. The movie shows how initially the Japanese and American cultures clash on what is expected from workers and management. The clash nearly crashes the opportunity for both the town and the car company, but in the end both Japanese and American workers learn their time for "doing" is now because to wait would mean failure for both.

The job seeker needs to look at the time for doing as every minute of every day because once the time is lost it can never be recovered. By always using time wisely by doing something focused on the job search the job seeker moves closer to their next opportunity.

1. Do you sometimes feel time is not on your side?
2. What hurdles do you face on a daily basis when it comes to time management?
3. What would you do in order to gain better time management skills?
4. How do you want to move forward to a time where you can better manage your job search time?

Prayer
Lord, remind me every day to continue to do my best in every situation. Please be gentle but firm, and remind me of the things most important in my life. I am not perfect, and I would never admit to thinking I was, but there are things I must do better. You know what they are, help me to improve upon them. Amen.

The Road To Rainbow Valley

In Genesis God promises Abraham land and many descendants, and the land came to be known as the "Promised Land". Getting to the "Promised Land" and staying there became a major challenge for the children of Israel. Nearly five hundred years after Abraham heard the promise Moses and the children of Israel departed Egypt for the "Promised Land", but it took forty (40) years in the Sinai before they reached the "Promised Land". Along the way the children of Israel had to not only prepare themselves as a free people but also receive the Ten Commandments through Moses, who received them from God. The Second Covenant between God and the children of Israel declared God would not abandon the children of Israel so long as the children of Israel adhered to God's Commandants and Law. The Second Covenant gets reaffirmed to David and Solomon as follows:

> and I will not again remove the foot of Israel from the land which I have appointed for your fathers — only if they are careful to do all that I have commanded them, according to the whole law and the statutes and the ordinances by the hand of Moses. (2 Chronicles 33:8)

In time the "Promised Land" became not just a dream and promise but the destination for the children of Israel. The "Promised Land" is a place the children of Israel were supposed to hold for a thousand generations.

Both the 1947 Broadway production and the 1968 film a musical titled "Finian's Rainbow" present the story of modern day wanderer and immigrant from Ireland named Finian McLonergan (Fred Astaire in the film). Finian is searching for a new home in America and he finds it in a place called Rainbow Valley. Of course, Finian has brought along his daughter Sharon (Petula Clark in the film), who is looking for a husband, and leprechaun's pot of gold, which he plans to bury close to Fort Know where it will grow and multiply. Rainbow Valley is far from ideal, but Sharon meets a young man full of ambition and dreams of a better future for himself, his family and his neighbors. The leprechaun's pot of gold generates complications for all, including Og the leprechaun (Tommy Steele in the film), who is growing taller and becoming mortal. "Finian's Rainbow" includes many wonderful songs including "Old Devil Moon", "Something Sort of Grandish", "If This Isn't Love", "Necessity","That Great 'Come-and-Get-It' Day", but a song titled "Look To The Rainbow" sums up the full meaning of the show. The chorus of "Look To The Rainbow" includes the following:

> Look to the rainbow. Follow the fellow who follows a dream.

Every job seeker is on their own quest not only to find their equivalent of Rainbow Valley but also to be the fellow in search of a realized dream. The road to a job seeker's Rainbow Valley may be long and cover many peaks and lows. The job seeker's Rainbow Valley may not be ideal, but it will provide a destination worthy of the promise and the dream because it will become the job seeker's new home away from the wilderness.

1. Where is your own Rainbow Valley?
2. What peaks and lows have you encountered along the road to your Rainbow Valley?
3. What have you done to strengthen your resolve to complete the journey to your Rainbow Valley?
4. Have you found help along the road to your Rainbow Valley in the form of new faith and friends?

Prayer

Lord, be our guide and our protector on the journey we have undertaken. Watch over us. Protect us from the pitfalls of despair along the way. Keep us free from harm to body and soul. Lord, support us with your grace when we are tired. Help us be patient in any trouble which may come our way. I pray we all safely reach our destination. Keep us always mindful of your presence and love. Blessed are you, Lord our God, you who hear our prayers. Amen.

Embrace The Bright Side Of Life

Joy or the ability to embrace the bright side of life would seem to be the natural imperative of faith both in the Old and New Testament. Throughout the Bible those seeking joy even amidst the most horrendous of circumstances are the ones most likely to find what they seek while those seemingly resigned to their fate remain unfulfilled and doomed to suffer the worst possible outcome for their experiences. Here are some clear words of joyful scripture:

Therefore my heart is glad, and my glory rejoices; my flesh also will rest in hope. (Psalm 16:9)

For His anger is but for a moment, His favor is for life; Weeping may endure for a night, but joy comes in the morning. (Psalm 30:5)

The hope of the righteous will be gladness, but the expectation of the wicked will perish. (Proverbs 10:28)

For you shall go out with joy, and be led out with peace; The mountains and the hills shall break forth into singing before you, and all the trees of the field shall clap their hands. (Isaiah 55:12)

These things I have spoken to you, that in Me you may have peace. In the world you will have tribulation, be of good cheer, I have overcome the world. (John 16:33)

Now may God of hope fill you with all joy and peace in believing, that you may abound in hope by the power of the Holy Spirit. (Romans 15:13)

My brethren, count it all joy when you fall into various trials. (James 1:2)

In the span of nearly fifty-one (51 years) Suzanne Marie Ciptak certainly knew how to embrace the bright side of life even though facing the toughest of life encounters repeatedly throughout the last decade of her life. When her husband John passed away in 2008 Suzanne decided to change careers and pursue a degree in social work in order to help abused children. She began to volunteer as a Guardian Ad Litem. Her life direction was challenged in 2009 when she was diagnosed with breast cancer, but through the surgery and chemotherapy she continued her studies and volunteer work. When her cancer spread and left her blind Suzanne remained resilient. She attended the Tampa Lighthouse for the Blind so she could remain living independently, and she adopted a retriever during her training at the Southwest Guide Dog School. Through it all she sang every day, remembered birthdays, always asked how everyone else was doing, and gave to charity. On January 22, 2014 she returned to God, but not without leaving a legacy of joy for all she meet along her path.

Job seekers make a decision each and every day regarding whether they will embrace or reject the bright side of life. Those choosing to embrace the bright side of life will be strengthened by the power of the Holy Spirit.

1. Have you embraced the bright side of life in spite of the tumult around you?
2. What do you do on a regular basis to hold your embrace on the bright side of life?
3. Have you found help along the way in maintaining your embrace of the bright side of life?

Prayer
As we continue our job search we bring Your presence with us. We acknowledge Your power over all that will be spoken, thought, decided, and done during these times. We thank You for the gifts You have blessed us with. When we are confused guide us. When we are burned out infuse us with the light of the Holy Spirit. Amen.

Old Dogs Can Still Hunt

Some of the most interesting parts of the Bible chronicle the lives of men and women considered to be "old dogs" by any standard or measurement. Creating a list of individuals achieving great accomplishments regardless of their age is exciting because it reveals evidence there is little or no link between age and the ability to achieve. How many people reading the Bible can overlook or forget about the accomplishments of Enoch, Noah, Abraham, Moses, Aaron, Joshua, Lamech, Noah's wife, Sarah, Miriam, Rebecca, Deborah the Nurse, Deborah the Judge or Anna the Prophetess.

A few of the accomplished older characters in the Bible may not be as familiar as others, but their roles are nonetheless important. For example, without Miriam there to place Moses in the Nile to be saved by Pharaoh's daughter Moses would surely have been killed. It was Miriam who suggested the princess take Yocheved as the child's nurse, which ensured the infant Moses would be familiar with his background as a Hebrew. Miriam is also known as a prophetess who sang a brief victory song after Pharaoh's army was drowned in the Red Sea.

> Then Miriam the prophetess, the sister of Aaron, took the timbrel in her hand; and all the women went out after her with timbrels and with dances. And Miriam answered them: Sing to the Lord, For He has triumphed gloriously! The horse and its rider He has thrown into the sea! (Exodus 15:20-21)

Deborah the Nurse, who is an elderly nurse, is dispatched by Rebecca to tell Jacob it is safe to return home after being away from home for 22 years. And, Deborah the Judge, who is the only female judge mentioned in the Bible, led a successful counterattack against the forces of Jabin King of Canaan and his military commander Sisera. The description of the battle is detailed in Chapter 5 of Judges, and the passage is often called "The Song of Deborah".

Finally, it was Anna the Prophetess who prophesied about Jesus at the Temple of Jerusalem at his presentation by speaking of Jesus and the redemption of Jerusalem. She was 84 at the time.

Throughout the Bible a person's age presents few barriers when there was a mission to be accomplished or a message to be delivered. The Bible shows many ways for people advanced in age to provide service to others even when such service comes with hardship.

In the job market today many job seekers are viewed as "old dogs" even when they are, in fact, quite young in years. In many professions a job seeker may be considered "over-qualified" whenever they have more than the number of years experience required for the position. The perception a job seeker as "over-qualified" provides a hurdle for many job seekers to overcome, but the job seeker must always bear in mind it is in their best interest to never sell themselves short or abandon hope for getting a position using the best combination of their skills rather than simply accepting a position using a minor set of their skills.

1. Which Bible character best illustrates the ability to accomplish much even in later years?
2. Are you able to keep your focus on presenting your best skills to prospective employers?
3. Have you found ways to expand your skill set using your experience and existing skills?
4. How do you answer when an interviewer states you might be "over-qualified" for a position?

Prayer

Lord, keep us ever mindful of the skills we have mastered while giving us the awareness of the necessity for ever expanding our knowledge and skills. Give us the strength to never simply accept age as anything more than a number, especially when it comes to the search for the position You have already envisioned for our next step in life. Be with us along the way to fulfill your hope for our future in Your service to each other and You. Amen.

Taking Advantage Of The Waiting Game

Nobody likes the waiting game. Examples of the waiting game are seen throughout the Bible. In most situations the waiting time includes an effort to take advantage of the waiting time. Think of Noah, who had been warned by God of a coming flood, using a period of waiting to build an ark to save his family and two of every living thing. Think of Moses and the children of Israel, who spent forty years in the desert on their way to the Promised Land, using the waiting time to prepare themselves as a free people and to receive the Second Covenant. In a very real sense the life of Jesus is a waiting time for Him, and he uses the waiting time to great advantage for the purpose of finding and then preparing his Apostles and disciples for the time after his departure. At His Ascension the Lord lets all present know of the coming time of waiting while adding it will be their duty to take advantage of the time of waiting.

> Therefore, when they had come together, they asked Him, saying, "Lord, will You at this time restore the kingdom to Israel?" And He said to them, "It is not for you to know times or seasons which the Father has put in His own authority. But you shall receive power when the Holy Spirit has come upon you; and you shall be witnesses to Me in Jerusalem, and in all Judea and Samaria, and to the end of the earth." (Acts 1:6-8)

Daniel Eugene "Rudy" Ruettiger, who was the third of fourteen children, had a dream of playing for the Notre Dame Fighting Irish football team despite being only 5'6" tall and weighing just 185 pounds. At the time Rudy entered Notre Dame Ara Parseghian, who was head coach, encouraged walk-on players. Amazingly, Rudy earned a spot on the Notre Dame scout team, which was a practice squad setup to act as the stand-in for the opponent the varsity team during practice. Rudy took a beating at every practice session and continued his studies at Notre Dame, but he still hadn't achieved his dream of running through the tunnel on game day and actually playing in a scheduled game. At the end of his Junior year Rudy thought he would get a chance to play in an actual game as Senior, but Ara Parseghian stepped down as head coach and was replaced by Dan Devine.

On November 8, 1975, which was the last home game of the season, Rudy finally saw his dream come true when Dan Devine put him in the game against Georgia Tech. Devine put Rudy on the field for what Devine thought would be the last play of the game, and Rudy recorded a sack. Rudy is the first of only two players in Notre Dame football history to be carried off the field by fellow players.

The most notable quote from the 1993 movie titled "Rudy" is about what Rudy did while waiting.

You're 5 foot nothin', 100 and nothin', and you have barely a speck of athletic ability. And you hung in there with the best college football players in the land for 2 years. And you're gonna walk outta here with a degree from the University of Notre Dame. In this life, you don't have to prove nothin' to nobody but yourself. And after what you've gone through, if you haven't done that by now, it ain't gonna never happen. Now go on back.

1. Who else either has shown or must show they take advantage of the waiting game?
2. Are you doing all you could do to take advantage of the job search waiting game?
3. What steps do you take to keep your job search funnel full during the waiting game?
4. What do you need to learn to take better advantage of the waiting game?

Prayer

Lord, our minds are racing with possibilities as we wait for the successful outcome of our job search. Quiet our minds and lessen our anxiety during this time of waiting. Give us the strength and vision to find ways to take advantage of the wait not only for our own needs but also for the needs of others. Amen.

Beyond Horseshoes And Hand Grenades

Everybody has heard of the phrase "close only counts in horseshoes and hand grenades", but they forget close always counts with the Holy Spirit.

But the manifestation of the Spirit is given to each one for the profit of all: for to one is given the word of wisdom through the Spirit, to another the word of knowledge through the same Spirit, to another faith by the same Spirit, to another gifts of healings by the same Spirit, to another the working of miracles, to another prophecy, to another discerning of spirits, to another different kinds of tongues, to another the interpretation of tongues. But one and the same Spirit works all these things, distributing to each other individually as He wills. For as the body is one and has many members, but all the members of that one body, being many, are one body, so also is Christ. For by one Spirit we were all baptized into one body – whether Jews, Greeks, whether slaves or free – and have all been made to drink into one Spirit. (1 Corinthians 12: 7-13)

Regardless of where a person goes they are always close to the Holy Spirit. If they are a believer, the Holy Spirit is inside them. In all things the Holy Spirit is present for the purpose of delivering help and guidance.

Likewise the Spirit also helps in our weaknesses. For we do not know what we should pray for as we ought, but the Spirit Himself makes intercession for us with groanings which cannot be uttered. (Romans 8:26-27)

Throughout history there has been times where it was clear there was an intercession by the Holy Spirit, especially at times when it would have been so easy for the situation to turn out very badly for countless millions of people around the globe. Think of how many things could have gone terribly wrong on

D-Day or just think about what would have happened had even a few more things on had gone wrong on D-Day as Allied forces made their way across the beaches and into French territory. Movies like "The Longest Day" (1962) or "Saving Private Ryan" (1998) make it a little easier to visualize just a portion of what happened during the D-Day invasion. The outcome of World War II might have been very different, but somehow through all the energy, effort, pain and suffering the tide turned in favor of the Allies.

The job seeker may feel alone and forgotten while thinking they may never get to the point where they will receive a job offer, but all along the way they are always close to the Holy Spirit whether or not they acknowledge the presence of the Holy Spirit. Intercessions by the Holy Spirit reach the job seeker in many ways, but the best outcome is realized when the job seeker heeds the nudge provided by the intercession.

1. Do you feel the power of the Holy Spirit in your daily life?
2. Can you feel the intercession of the Holy Spirit in your job search?
3. What can job seekers do to open up more to the power of the Holy Spirit?
4. What would you say to a job seeker that would help them get in touch with the Holy Spirit?

Prayer
O God, send forth your Holy Spirit into my heart that I may perceive, into my mind that I may remember, and into my soul that I may meditate. Inspire me to speak with piety, holiness, tenderness and mercy. Teach, guide and direct my thoughts and senses from beginning to end. May your grace ever help and correct me, and may I be strengthened now with wisdom from on high, for the sake of your infinite mercy. Amen. (Saint Anthony of Padua)

What Do We Do Now?

One of the most frightening questions anybody can hear is, "What do we do now?". After seeing the Ascension of Jesus and receiving the gift of the Holy Spirit the disciples surely asked one another the question, and the next steps for Christianity unfold as each disciple moves out into the world to do the will of the Lord.

> And Jesus came and spoke to them, saying, "All authority has been given to Me in heaven and on earth. Go therefore and make disciples of all the nations, baptize them in the name of the Father and of the Son and of the Holy Spirit, teaching them to observe all things that I have commanded you, and lo, I am with you always, even to the end of the age."
> (Matthew 28: 18-20)

From the perspective of the disciples the task ahead following the Ascension of Jesus and the receipt of the Holy Spirit surely seemed beyond daunting to the point of impossibility, but the disciples had only just received the Holy Spirit. The disciples could not have known the true power of the Holy Spirit. The disciples could not have known the Holy Spirit would lead people to the truth and reality of God in Christ without propagandizing religious information and doctrinal data. The disciples could not have known the Holy Spirit would reveal what was to come without speculating calculations of timetables. The disciples could not have possibly known the Holy Spirit would glorify Jesus and reveal the nature of the Lord to the people without concentrating just on the Lord. In short, the disciples did not know the gift of the Holy Spirit had already provided them with all they needed for their work spreading the Gospel. As with the first disciples, the time when Christians miss the advantage of the Holy Spirit is when they are dreary, discouraged and generally down in the mouth.

From the very beginning of a job search the job seeker can feel alone and unsure about what they must do to move forward with the task ahead of them. Many job seekers feel so unnerved by what they must do during their job search campaign they forget to tap not only their skills but also the advantage given by the Holy Spirit. When the job seeker allows the Holy Spirit to intercede in the progress of the job search the job seeker suddenly begins to see the path become brighter, and the steps along the way seem more secure. By any measure the job seeker is engaged in a journey requiring every ounce of skill and energy the job seeker can muster, but by accepting and acknowledging the advantage of the Holy Spirit the journey will lead to success.

1. Do you sometimes wake up thinking you have difficulty deciding what to do during the day?
2. Do you frequently feel dreary, discouraged and generally down in the mouth?
3. What gets you back on track with your job search?
4. What can job seekers do to more easily recognize the advantage of the Holy Spirit?

Prayer
Holy Spirit of all wisdom and understanding come to us now and enlighten our minds so we may perceive the mysteries of the universe in relation to all eternity. Holy Spirit of right judgment and courage, guide us now and and forever to renew our decision to follow Lord's way of love. Holy Spirit of knowledge and reverence, help us now to see the everlasting value of justice and mercy in our everyday dealings with each another. May we all respect life as we work through our time as a job seeker. Holy Spirit give us the spark to fuel our faith, the hope and love to attain new action each day. Holy Spirit fill our lives with joy, wonder and awe in your presence. Amen.

Of Bolles' Boxes, Maps, Mission, And Parachutes

When most people think of Richard Bolles they immediately think of his book titled "What Color is Your Parachute?". What most folks don't know is Richard Bolles' presence in the world of job hunting and life choices extends well beyond his iconic job search primer. Bolles other writings include "The Job-Hunter's Survival Guide: How to Find Hope and Rewarding Work, Even When There Are No Jobs (2009)", "The New Quick Job-Hunting Map" (2009), and "The Three Boxes of Life, and How to Get Out of Them: An Introduction to Life/Work Planning" (1981), but none is more appropriate for a faith-based job search than "How to Find Your Mission in Life" (2005) because it provides the faith-based context for each of his other works.

Indeed, the task of finding a Mission in life is not only what Jesus asks of everyone but also it is the task He so wonderfully illustrated with His own life and works.

Most assuredly, I say to you, he who believes in Me, the works that I do he will do also, and greater works than these he will do, because I go to My Father. (John 14:12)

Jesus' mission and identification with man is clear. Of equal importance is how Jesus spoke of His time on Earth.

I came forth from the Father and have come into the world. Again, I leave the world and go to the Father. (John 16:28)

In the strictest sense the time between birth and the time to go back to the Father is the "In Between Time".

According to Bolles there are three (3) parts to a person's Mission in life as follows:

1) to seek to stand hour by hour in the conscious presence of God, the One from whom your Mission is derived; 2) to do what you can moment by moment, day by day, step by step, to make this world a better place — following the leading and guidance of God's Spirit within you and around you; and, 3) to exercise that Talent which you particularly came to Earth to use in those place(s) or setting(s) which God has caused to appeal to you most, and those purposes which God most needs to be done in the world.

The first and second part in finding a person's Mission in life is shared by all, but the third is unique to each person. Through a step-by-step process each person finds the third part of their Mission, and at the end of a successful job search Bolles would hope every job seeker would be able to say,

Life has deep meaning to me, now. I have discovered more than my ideal job; I have found my Mission, and the reason why I am here on Earth.

1. Did you know there was more to Bolles than simply his book on parachutes?
2. Does the task of finding you Mission in life add context to your job search?
3. What aspects of the step-by-step process of a job search giving you the most trouble?
4. Where have you gone to get help with making progress with your job search?

Prayer
Lord be with us today and every day as we continue our job search. Lead us to find our mission in life and guide us along the road of discovery leading us to our ideal job. Give us strength to stay the course until we can truthfully declare to all we have found or mission on Earth and know exactly why we are here to accomplish the purpose most needed for our special talents. Amen.

Sowing Seeds To Grow A Working Network

The Parable of the Sower appears in each of the Synoptic Gospels and the non-canonical Gospel of Thomas. In each telling of the Parable of the Sower Jesus describes what happens when a farmer's seeds fall on different types of ground.

> On the same day Jesus went out of the house and sat by the sea. And great multitudes were gathered together to Him, so that He got into a boat and sat; and the whole multitude stood on the shore. Then He spoke many things to them in parables, saying: "Behold, a sower went out to sow. And as he sowed, some seed fell by the wayside; and the birds came and devoured them. Some fell on stony places, where they did not have much earth; and they immediately sprang up because they had no depth of earth. But when the sun was up they were scorched, and because they had no root they withered away. And some fell among the thorns, and the thorns sprang up and choked them. But others fell on good ground and yielded a crop: some a hundredfold, some sixty, some thirty."
> (Matthew 13:1-8)

Job seekers need to spend a part of each day sowing seeds to grow a working network, and they must do so with a limited number of seeds, which means they must always be careful about where they cast their seeds. As with the sower described in the Parable of the Sower, the job seeker faces perils similar to those described by Jesus.

LinkedIn affords each member 3,000 invitations they can use to invite people they know to join their LinkedIn network, which means those 3,000 invitations are very much like the seeds the sower has at the beginning of the Parable of the Sower. How the LinkedIn member uses the 3,000 invitations has a great bearing on the degree of success they will have in growing a working LinkedIn network.

If the LinkedIn member sends out invitations to people they clearly do not know, they are like the sower's seeds falling by the wayside where they were eaten by birds. On LinkedIn sending invitations out to people the member does not know not only produces poor results but also the practice can lead to having the member's account restricted in the event just five (5) people receiving such invitations respond to the invitation by clicking the "I Don't Know" option.

If the LinkedIn member sends out invitations only to people showing "LION" (LinkedIn Open Networker) on their profile, the result is very much like the sower's seeds falling on stony places. The invitations will be accepted by the recipient, but in most cases there is very little substance to such connections. In the light of day the recipient of such invitations cannot be counted on as a reliable LinkedIn connection because they have no real knowledge of the sender.

If the LinkedIn member sends out invitations to recruiters, hiring managers, and headhunters, they are like the sower's seeds falling among the thorns because all too often such members are more interested in the other member's connections than in the actual member, especially when it comes to being a truly good connection.

If, on the other hand, the member chooses who to send an invitation with care and consideration, the results are like the sower's seeds falling on good ground, and they will yield good results, which may be beyond the member's initial expectations.

1. Have you given much consideration to how best to use your LinkedIn invitations?
2. What has been your experience with sending out invitations to open networkers and recruiters?
3. Are you connected with all of the members of the job seeker groups you have joined?

4. What do you need to learn in order to be better at growing a working network?

Prayer
Lord, we pray to you asking for the blessing of a true friend. We are grateful for all you have blessed us with. We ask your blessing for us and those around us and that you grant us the opportunity to make a positive difference in the lives of all those we touch. In your name. Amen.

Jacob's Ladder Experience For Job Seekers

Jacob's ladder experience in Genesis provides one of the most iconic images found anywhere in the Bible. The scene has been rendered using everything from a simple ladder to a huge spiral staircase ascending to the heavens.

In any event Jacob was on what amounted to a journey to save his life because his mother Rebekah had told him to flee his home in Beersheba and go to her brother Laban's house in Haran because Rebekah had overheard Jacob's twin brother Esau say he was going to kill Jacob.

During the journey to Haran Jacob stopped to sleep one evening after sunset in what seems to be the middle of the desert. Using only a stone as his pillow he fell asleep and had a dream.

Jacob went out from Beersheba and went toward Haran. So he came to a certain place and stayed there all night, because the sun had set. And he took one of the stones of that place and put it at his head, and he lay down in that place to sleep. Then he dreamed and behold, a ladder was set up on the earth, and its top reached to heaven; and there the angels of God were ascending and descending on it. And behold, the Lord stood above it and said: I am the Lord God of Abraham your father and the God of Isaac; the land on which you lie I will give to you and your descendants. Also your descendants shall be as the dust of the earth; you shall spread abroad to the west and the east, to the north and the south; and in you and in your seed all the families of the earth shall be blessed. Behold, I am with you and will keep you wherever you go, and will bring you back to this land; for I will not leave you until I have done what I have spoken to you. Then Jacob awoke from his sleep and said, "Surely the Lord is in this place, and I did not know it.
(Genesis 28: 10-16)

Each night as a job seeker settles for the evening they may feel just as Jacob did in the desert, and they may feel like they are putting their head on a rock as they lay down for a night of sleep.

As the job seeker fades off to sleep, their mind may be filled with heavy thoughts regarding what to do next and where they will be by the end of the next day, next week or next month. But, as each job seeker awakes the next morning they should remind themselves of Jacob's revelation and say to themselves, "Surely the Lord is in this place, and I did not know it."

Indeed, wherever the job seeker goes and whatever the job seeker does they should always remember God is with them and will keep them wherever they go, and God will bring the job seeker back from the desert of unemployment to a better place and situation. As with Jacob, the job seeker must always keep the vision of God's promise in mind through each step along their path during their journey as a job seeker.

1. Do you sometimes feel like your bed pillow is hard as a rock after a particularly tough day?
2. Do you frequently remind yourself of God's presence throughout the day?
3. What methods have you used to remind yourself of God's presence in your life as a job seeker?
4. Have you ever taken the time to remind others of God's presence in their life as a job seeker?

Prayer
Search me, O God, and know my heart; Try me, and know my anxieties; And see if there is any wicked way in me, And lead me in the way everlasting. Amen. (Psalm 139: 23-24)

Are You Planting Seeds Or Just Empty Jars?

Matthew 13 includes many parables illustrating faith, heaven, and spiritual growth, but the parable of the mustard seed provides special meaning for job seekers not so much for what it says but for what it describes.

> Another parable He put forth to them saying, "The Kingdom of heaven is like a mustard seed, which a man took and sowed in his field, which indeed is the least of all the seeds; but when it is grown it is greater than the herbs and becomes a tree, so that the birds of the air come and nest in its branches." (Matthew 13:31-32)

In a 20th century version of the parable of the mustard seed a new character is added in the guise of a small young boy. Upon first hearing the parable of the mustard seed as a Gospel reading in Church a very young boy becomes intrigued. He decides to put the parable of the mustard seed to the test with a plan to grow a mustard tree. All might have turned out better but for one small detail. The young boy was particularly fond of "French's Mustard", which was sold in grocery stores at the time in small glass jars. He decided the best thing to grow would be some "French's Mustard". The young planter came to the conclusion the jar was the "seed" because it seemed to be the source for the mustard. He salvaged a "French's Mustard" jar and planted it in a place where he thought it would be sure to grow. He waited and waited for the mustard tree to sprout and grow into a mighty tree, but surprisingly for him nothing happened. It wasn't until much later the young boy learned the reason for his lack of success as a planter, but in learning the cause of his lack of success he also learned a very important lesson in life worth remembering and sharing with all.

The lesson learned by the young boy was as follows:

> "Don't expect a mustard tree unless you are sure you have sowed the proper seed."

Every day the job seeker makes decisions regarding their job search, and with each decision they run the risk of planting a "mustard jar" when they intend to be planting a "mustard seed". For the job seeker most of their decisions are related to making a good first impression, which means each contact with a potential employer must be the equivalent of a "mustard seed" because any employer receiving the equivalent of a "mustard jar" will be very unlikely to give the job seeker another opportunity. Thus, the job seeker must always take the time to ensure what they plant is, indeed, what they truly want to sow.

Two of the most important steps in a job seeker's search for new employment are planning and goal setting because without the planning and a focus on setting smart goals the whole job search experience is going to be even more frustrating than it would be in the best of circumstances. The worst part of failing to plan and set smart goals for a job seeker is the time lost trying to conduct a job search without planning and smart goal setting.

1. Do you sometimes feel like you are planting mustard jars rather than mustard seeds?
2. How much time do you spend planning your job search and setting smart goals?
3. What methods have you used to keep yourself on plan with your smart goals?
4. How much of your time have spent helping others do a better job with their job search?

Prayer
Lord, the parable of the mustard seed shows us what can come from humble beginnings. We thank you for Your encouragement to maintain our faith and service to You. We need motivation because of the world presents many ways for us to stray. Lord, continue to enlighten us and strengthen us for all future battles. Help us persevere to the end, to our final breaths. Amen.

Building An Accomplishments Based Resume

Throughout the Bible accomplishments become a part of the ongoing narrative. Of course, the descriptions of specific deeds and accomplishments add detail about the person involved, but also the detail regarding specific accomplishments becomes the core message for the passage and, indeed, what we remember about the person. Here are a couple examples taken from different parts of the Bible.

Now both Jesus and His disciples were invited to the wedding. And when they ran out of wine, the mother of Jesus said to Him, "They have no wine." Jesus said to her, "Woman what does your concern have to do with Me? My hour has not yet come". His mother said to the servants, "Whatever He says to you do it." Now there were set there six waterpots of stone, according to the manner of purification of the Jews, containing twenty or thirty gallons apiece. Jesus said to them, "Fill the waterpots with water." And they filled them up to the brim. And He said to them, "Draw some out now, and take it to the master of the feast." And they took it. When the master of the feast had tasted the water that was made wine, and did not know where it came from (but the servants who had drawn the water knew), the master of the feast called the bridegroom. And he said to him, "Every man at the beginning sets out the good wine, and when the guests have well drunk, then the inferior. You have kept the good wine until now." This beginning of signs Jesus did in Cana of Galilee, and manifested His glory; and His disciples believed in Him. (John 2:2-11)

When it was evening, His disciples came to Him, saying, "This is a deserted place, and the hour is already late. Send the multitudes away, that they may go into the villages and buy themselves food." But Jesus said to them, "They do not need to go away. You give them something to eat." And they said to Him, "We have here only five loaves and two fish." He said, "Bring them here to Me." Then He commanded the multitudes to sit down on the grass. And He took the five loaves and the two fish, and looking up to heaven, He blessed and broke and gave the loaves to the disciples; and the disciples gave to the multitudes. So they all ate and were filled, and they took up twelve baskets full of the fragments that remained. Now those who had eaten were about five thousand men, besides women and children. (Matthew 14:15-21)

There are many other places in the Bible where accomplishments are used to truly make the Word jump off the page, but there are many more things described in the Bible much less exciting or immediately memorable. The Bible includes things like "begets", rules, location descriptions, along with other detail as part of the full content of the Bible. A person may be attracted to Bible because of the accomplishments they remember, but when they return to the Bible they wind up learning much more than they might have imagined. The same is true when a job seeker uses memorable accomplishments when presenting themselves during a job search. Once a job seeker gains an employer's attention they gain the opportunity to tell them more about themselves and in doing so present a case for getting hired.

1. What accomplishments from the Bible bring you back to the Bible again and again?
2. Does your resume and introduction contain more "begets" than "accomplishments"?
3. What do you need to put more focus on your "accomplishments" than "begets"?

Prayer
Lord, help us define our accomplishments in life even though we have buried them in a sea of begets. Lead us to the career which will enable us to do God's will, which will bring us joy and take away anxiety and despair. Please open the doors necessary for us to move forward in a positive light. Amen.

Never Let Yourself Be Swamped

As much as anything else the Bible reveals both the how and why people need to not let themselves be swamped by the circumstances of life to the point they forget about the presence of God in their life. In both the Old Testament and New Testament there are many examples of people letting themselves get swamped by life events along with God's scriptural response. Here are a few examples:

And those who know Your name will put their trust in You; For You, Lord, have not forsaken those who seek You. (Psalm 9:10)

And Peter answered Him and said, "Lord, if it is You, command me to come to You on the water." So He said, "Come." And when Peter had come down out of the boat, he walked on the water to go to Jesus. But when he saw that the wind was boisterous, he was afraid; and beginning to sink he cried out, saying, "Lord, save me!" And immediately Jesus stretched out His hand and caught him, and said to him, "O you of little faith, why did you doubt?" (Matthew 14:28-31)

For I consider that the sufferings of this present time are not worthy to be compared with the glory which shall be revealed to us. (Romans 8:18)

No temptation has overtaken you except such as is common to man; but God is faithful, who will not allow you to be tempted beyond what you are able, but with the temptation will also make the way of escape, that you may be able to bear it. (1 Corinthians 10:13)

Blessed is the man who endures temptation; for when he has been approved, he will receive the crown of life which the Lord has promised to those who love Him. Let no one say when he is tempted, "I am tempted by God"; for God cannot be tempted by evil, nor does

He Himself tempt anyone. But each one is tempted
when he is drawn away by his own desires and enticed.
(James 1:12-14)

Therefore submit to God. Resist the devil and he will
flee from you. (James 4:7)

On a daily basis the whole job search journey can be
daunting to the point where the job seeker wants to throw up
their hands while feeling they are totally abandoned, but it is at
those times the job seeker must stop and listen to their heart
while reminding themselves of the fact they are not alone in
their time of need. It is at such times the job seeker must
dismiss whatever is drawing them away from their faith and
reach out for the hand outstretched from the Lord. Bear in
mind Lord's outstretched hand may be the hand of a close
friend, family member or even the hand of a stranger.

Of course, there will be times when a job seeker will be
called upon to be the one reaching out the hand to help
someone else whether they be another job seeker or someone
else in need. Never hesitate to reach out because what you do
at such times are sure to be part of His plan for us all.

1. When you feel swamped do you recognize you
   are being tempted to stray from your job
   search?
2. What temptations do you face in your job
   search?
3. What do you need to pull yourself back to
   safety when you begin to feel swamped?
4. How would you help someone feeling
   swamped?

Prayer
Lord, we come to you swamped with the weight of our
struggles. Take away our fears. We wish to walk with You.
Heal us Lord and hold us close. Help us trust Your wisdom is
greater than ours. Amen.

God's Presence Is Everywhere And Always With You

God is omnipresent. He is everywhere continuously and simultaneously throughout the whole of creation. He is always there for everyone even when someone feels utterly and completely alone in the world. Specific mention of the presence of God appears throughout the Bible, and in every instance there can be no doubt the presence is for everyone regardless of their condition or situation. Here are some examples:

And He said, "My Presence will go with you, and I will give you rest." (Exodus 33:14)

You will show me the path of life; In Your presence is fullness of joy. (Psalm 16:11)

Do not cast me away from Your presence, And do not take Your Holy Spirit from me. (Psalm 51:11)

And He has made from one blood every nation of men to dwell on all the face of the earth, and has determined their preappointed times and the boundaries of their dwellings, so that they should seek the Lord, in the hope that they should seek the Lord, in the hope they might grope for Him and find Him, though He is not far from each of us; for in Him we live and move and have our being, as also some of your own poets have said, "For we are also His offspring." (Acts 17:26-28)

Paulo Coelho's most famous novel titled "The Alchemist" has sold over 65 million copies, and it has been translated into 80 different languages. "The Alchemist" is one of the best-selling books in history, but it didn't start off as a resounding success for the author. On August 14, 2014, Paulo Coelho gave a rare interview for Krista Tipplett's "On Being" radio broadcast. During the interview Paulo Coelho said it took a year to sell 900 copies. The original publisher gave the book back to Paulo Coelho saying they did not want to publish the book anymore. Paulo Coelho told Krista Tipplett his choice was to either move forward or die. He didn't mean physically die, but spiritually. At his lowest he thought of a sentence in "The Alchemist" and he said, "I have to honor my words. I have to be an example. I have to give an example. Did I write this? I did. So, what I'm going to do is I'm going to knock doors." The single sentence providing the inspiration is, "When a person really desires something, all the universe conspires to help that person to realize his dream." Another very telling quotation from "The Alchemist" is the following:

> People are afraid to pursue their most important dreams, because they feel that they don't deserve them, or that they'll be unable to achieve them.

Paulo Coelho never gave up on his dreams, and as of May 25, 2014 the novel reached its 303rd consecutive week on the "New York Times" bestseller list.

The job seeker's journey may seem like the loneliest journey, but at least once a day the job seeker would do well to think about the presence of God and Paulo Coelho's journey to success as an author.

1. Are there times when you cannot feel the presence of God?
2. What do you think about when you cannot feel the presence of God?
3. Why do you deserve to achieve your dreams?
4. What obstacles are in your path to achieving your dreams and what have you done to get past them?

Prayer

Lord, may we all be so bold as to invite You to enter our life today? We each acknowledge, Lord, that to have You in our being, We are most unworthy. But please know, Lord, that we are needy. Look into our hearts, and see the sincerity of our plea. If we find favor in Your eyes, let even the smallest morsel of Your presence stay with us. That will suffice, Lord. Amen.

Doing Your Best To Renew Your Mind

The Bible calls on the faithful to do many things along the path to being closer to God, but none can be more valuable than what each person does to renew their mind in ways bringing them closer to the perfect will of God. The call for such renewal is found in the Bible as follows:

> And do not be conformed to this world, but be transformed by the renewing of your mind, that you may prove what is that good and acceptable and perfect will of God (Romans 12:2)

The most interesting thing about the passage is there is no mention of when the process of renewing your mind ever ends, which means there was no intention the process should ever really end. To be true to the passage someone would have to work at renewing their mind a little bit every day. In fact, the mind receives new information each minute of every day.

There is always a stream of new information flowing to the mind. Of course, there should be much more to renewing the mind than simply being awake, and the more thought given to the task of renewal the better success can be made in getting to the good and acceptable and perfect will of God.

In 1999 Robin Williams starred in a movie titled "Bicentennial Man", which is based on a short story written by Isaac Asimov. Robin Williams plays the lead character, who is an android. The story begins when the android is delivered to the Martin family. Within a matter of days the family realizes they don't have an ordinary android because "Andrew" begins to experience emotions and creative thoughts.

"Andrew" spends an increasing amount of time developing his special talents while "Sir", who is technically "Andrew's" owner, allows "Andrew" to expand his skills. One of the skills "Andrew" develops is an ability to imagine an animal and then carve driftwood into a sculpture of the animal. He sells his carvings and soon he has a substantial income.

"Andrew's" goal is to become accepted as human and works to make himself more human in every way. Along the way he invents ways to help humans suffering from organ failures.

Eventually, he achieves his goal, and he is accepted as human. In becoming human he gave up what amounted to immortality.

People reading the passage from Romans, including job seekers, are encouraged to come closer to God by renewing their mind and by doing so move closer to the perfect will of God. The journey to attaining what is the best they can be according to the will of God will take a lifetime, but the journey brings them closer to God, who is their creator. Certainly a part of each day should be devoted to the task of being transformed by the renewing of the mind.

1. How are you working at the task of being transformed by the renewing of the mind?
2. What do you think about when planning how to move forward with your transformation?
3. What obstacles have you encountered along your journey of transformation?
4. Do you think you are doing everything you can to renew your mind?

Prayer
Lord, Your love calls us to be Your people. By sharing our diversity of gifts we share in Your mission. Lord, shape us into a community of faith and nourish us by Your word that we may grow in spirit. Through the power of Your Holy Spirit, help us that we, in turn, may help others. Form us all to be instruments of love, justice, and peace, and send us to proclaim Your work. Lord, renew us that we may renew the face of the earth. Amen.

Remove Obstacles By Casting Out Doubt

The major obstacle for building and holding faith is related to the level of doubt someone allows to linger in their mind. While the Lord's faith in humanity is limitless mere mortals often struggle from day-to-day getting their objectives accomplished because they continually create obstacles for themselves by thinking too much about why they can't get something done rather than getting something done.

The New Testament of the Bible provides two (2) excellent passages related to what someone can and can't do when they set themselves to a task.

"For assuredly, I say to you, whoever says to this mountain, 'Be removed and be cast into the sea,' and does not doubt in his heart, but believe that those things he says will be done, he will have whatever he says. Therefore I say to you, whatever things you ask when you pray, believe that you will receive them, and you will have them." (Mark 11:23-24)

From that time Jesus began to show to His disciples that He must go to Jerusalem, and suffer many things from the elders and chief priests and scribes, and be killed, and be raised the third day. Then Peter took Him aside and began to rebuke Him, saying, "Far be it from You, Lord; this shall not happen to You!" But He turned and said to Peter, "Get behind Me, Satan! You are an offense to Me, for you are not mindful of the things of God, but the things of men." (Matthew 16:21-23)

On October 1, 1986 a little girl was born without legs because of a birth defect. At the age of three (3) months the little girl was adopted by Gerald and Sharon Bricker, who already had three (3) boys. Sharon had prayed for someone who needed a home as badly as she wanted a daughter. The Brickers applied to adopt the little girl sight unseen. The little girl was named Jennifer, and she grew up in Hardinville, Illinois, which is a tiny unincorporated village with a population less than one hundred.

Both Gerald and Sharon Bricker said they would not limit Jennifer in what she might accomplish in life. As she grew, Jennifer was able to get around surprisingly well, and it wasn't long before Jennifer declared she wanted to be a tumbler. Starting on a trampoline, which she soon mastered, it wasn't long before she was on her school's tumbling team. Jennifer's idol was Dominique Moceanu, who is an Olympic gymnastic champion. Eventually Jennifer became the first handicapped high school tumbling champion in the state of Illinois.

At age sixteen (16) Jennifer asked her mom whether or not she knew anything about her natural Mother. Sharon tells Jennifer she does know something about her natural Mother, but she needs to sit down first. Jennifer's response was, "I am always sitting down, but maybe you need to sit down." It was then Sharon told her the last name of her natural Mother was Moceanu, which meant Dominique Moceanu was actually Jennifer's natural sister. Soon the sisters met, and Jennifer's family grew even more. Today Jennifer is an aerialist, acrobat, motivational speaker and TV personality all because she took "can't" out of her vocabulary and looked at her opportunities in life as "limitless".

Job seekers face many obstacles along their job search journey, but they need to remember the example of Jennifer Bricker, who wouldn't let "can't" keep her from reaching her dreams.

1. How often do you have feelings of doubt about your job search?
2. What do you do when you feel yourself becoming overburdened with doubt?
3. Who do you turn to for help when you begin to encounter the obstacle of doubt?

Prayer

O Christ Jesus, when all is darkness and we feel our weakness and helplessness, give us the sense of Your presence, Your love, and Your strength. Help us to have perfect trust in Your protecting love and strengthening power, so that nothing may frighten or worry us, for, living close to You, we shall see Your hand, Your purpose, Your will through all things. Amen
(St. Ignatius of Loyola)

Nobody Ever Said A Job Search Was Fair

The Bible clearly defines both the rewards of living a true and faithful life and the consequences of living a life of sin. However, there is really no place in the Bible where it is said life is fair. Perhaps the best outcome is in seeing the wicked receive the consequences for their sins, which is the case with the servant and the debt he owes his master coupled with how the servant treats those indebted to him.

> Then Peter came to Him and said, "Lord, how often shall my brother sin against me, and I forgive him? Up to seven times?" Jesus said to him, "I do not say to you up to seven times, but up to seventy times seven. Therefore the kingdom of heaven is like a certain king who wanted to settle accounts with his servants. And when he had begun to settle accounts, one was brought to him who owed him ten thousand talents. But he was not able to pay, his master commanded that he be sold, with his wife and children and all that he had, and that payment be made. The servant therefore fell down before him, saying, 'Master, have patience with me, and I will pay you all.' "Then the master of that servant was moved with compassion, released him, and forgave him the debt. But that servant went out and found one of his fellow servants who owed him a hundred denarii; and he laid hands on him and took him by the throat, saying, 'Pay me what you owe!' "So his fellow servant fell down at his feet and begged him, saying, 'Have patience with me and I will pay you all.' "And he would not, but went and threw him into prison till he should pay the debt. So when his fellow servants saw what had been done, they were very grieved, and came and told their master all that had been done. Then his master, after he had called him, said to him, 'You wicked servant! I forgave you all that debt because you begged me. Should you not also have had compassion on your fellow servant, just as I had pity on you?' "And his master was angry, and delivered

him to the torturers until he should pay all that was due to him. So My heavenly Father also will do to you if each of you, from his heart, does not forgive his brother his trespasses." (Matthew 18:21-35)

Being able to forgive may cleanse the soul, but for many the sting leaves a bitter and painful memory.

Perhaps the most bothersome example of the lack of fairness in the job search is in the job seekers inability to actually make a direct plea to a potential employer. It could happen when a resume doesn't lead to an interview or when an interview doesn't lead to a job offer. While the job seeker may forgive, they must still suffer the consequences of not achieving the desired results. In such cases where the job seeker feels there was a real fit the sting and disappointment can be even more painful.

The only rational option for a job seeker in such circumstances is to forgive and make the best of the experience in hopes they won't find themselves in a similar situation again and again throughout their job search. In the spiritual sense the better part of forgiveness comes when the forgiveness is coupled with a commitment to move on with the knowledge they had not yet found the position the Lord has intended for them to take.

1. Can you remember specific times when you felt the lack of fairness in your job search?
2. Have you been able to forgive others when you have felt the sting of unfairness in the job search?
3. Are you able to move on in light of unfairness in the job search and learn from such experiences?
4. What have you done to better benefit from the many setbacks associated with a job search?

Prayer

Lord, teach us to make the best of all the painful things in our life and help us to forgive the people who hurt us. Give us the wisdom to see beyond this moment, to understand and accept the deepest motivations that make people hurt other people. Give us the inner strength to heal and not to break, to comfort and not to destroy, to repay good for evil and love for hatred. Turn every experience into a spiritual well, from which we can draw drops of strength and wisdom. You are the only help we have and in You we put all our trust now and forever. Amen.

It's Never Too Late To Start

There are very few examples of a hiring event in the Bible, and fewer where there is much detail regarding a human resource issue such as compensation detailed. The best example of a hiring event in the Bible where compensation is a part of the narrative comes from the Gospel of Matthew. Everybody is familiar with the last verse of the passage, which is as follows:

"So the last will be first, and the first last. For many are called, but few are chosen" (Matthew 20:16)

Of course the hiring event is where Jesus compares the kingdom of heaven with what a landowner does while hiring laborers to harvest his vineyard. The narrative begins with the landowner going out early in the morning to hire laborers and agreeing on a daily wage with those hired. Throughout the day the landowner goes out to hire more laborers. He goes out to bring in more laborers at nine o'clock, noon, three o'clock, and finally again at five o'clock. At five o'clock he says to those he found, "Why are you standing here idle all day?" They say to him, "Because no one has hired us." His response is, "You also go into the vineyard."

When evening comes it is time to pay the laborers. The owner of the vineyard says to his manager, "Call the laborers and give them their pay, beginning with the last and then going to the first." When those hired about five o'clock come, each of them receives the usual daily wage. When the first come, they think they might receive more, but each of them also receives the usual daily wage. And when they receive it they grumble to the landowner saying, "These last worked only one hour, and you have made them equal to us who have borne the burden of the day and the scorching heat". The landowner replies to one of them, "Friend, I am doing you no wrong; did you not agree with me for the usual daily wage? Take what belongs to you and go; I choose to give to this last the same as I give to you. Am I not allowed to do what I choose with what belongs to me? Or are you envious because I am generous?"

The job seeker needs to view the narrative from the perspective of the last laborers hired during the day and ponder about what those last workers were doing earlier during the day when the landowner made his many earlier attempts to hire laborers. Where were these last workers? Also, the job seeker should ask whether or not there were others available for hire not even bothering to come outside and stand in the open. Don't job seekers act a lot like the laborers the landowner had to seek out from the start of the day until the very end of the day?

For the job seeker having spent a long time without work the offer of work should hold the same joy as might have been felt had they been hired earlier because by being hired they become not only amongst those called but also the chosen even while others doing nothing remain hidden in the shadows waiting to be chosen.

1. Can you remember specific times when you have not paid attention to the call from an employer?
2. Have you spent too much time lurking in the shadows while others make themselves available?
3. Do you have a workable goal and plan for making yourself more available to employers?
4. What have you done to ensure you are fully visible and available to employers?

Prayer
Lord, teach us to make the best of our time as a job seeker by not letting us miss those who might call for our services. Give us the strength to make ourselves available when a call comes. Enable us to stand steadfast always in full readiness for the call, and let us hear Your voice when the time is right. Amen.

Life, Liberty And The Pursuit Of Happiness

If someone were to go through the Bible from cover to cover and then give a single word to describe what they had found, "happy" would probably not be the first choice. Of course, there are many places in the Bible describing "life", "liberty" and the pursuit of "happiness", but many such references are obscured by arcane phrasing and language. For example,

A man had two sons, and he came to the first and said, "Son, go, work today in my vineyard." He answered and said, "I will not", but afterward he regretted it and went. Then he came to the second and said likewise. And he answered and said, "I go sir," but he did not go. Which of the two did the will of his father. (Matthew 21:28-31)

Surely each son took the path in pursuit of their own happiness, but only one did the will of his father.

Upon crossing the Jordan Moses says many things to the Israelites, including the following:

You shall not abhor an Edomite, for he is your brother. You shall not abhor an Egyptian, because you were an alien in his land. (Deuteronomy 23:7)

The Israelites were puzzled by the part about the Egyptians because they had escaped Egypt and the slavery it had held for them. What they didn't immediately understand was the importance of taking the anger and hatred of the Egyptians out of their minds because until the Egyptians were out of the Israelite's minds the fact they were out of Egypt alone would not give them the life, liberty and happiness they sought for themselves and their heirs.

In 2006 Will Smith starred in a movie titled "The Pursuit of Happyness". The movie is based on the true story of

Christopher Gardner. Christopher Gardner fails at a business venture, loses his wife, and faces hardship for both himself and his young son. Being either homeless or living in a flophouse with his young son his struggles seem to be in vain, but he finally lands an internship as a stockbroker trainee even though he has no experience in the field. His hard work pays off when he passes his stockbroker exam on the first try. Some of the thoughts going through Christopher Gardner's mind include the following:

> You got a dream... You gotta protect it. People can't do somethin' themselves, they wanna tell you you can't do it. If you want somethin', go get it. Period.

> It was right then that I started thinking about Thomas Jefferson on the Declaration of Independence and the part about our right to life, liberty, and the pursuit of happiness. And I remember thinking how did he know to put the pursuit part in there? That maybe happiness is something that we can only pursue and maybe we can actually never have it. No matter what. How did he know that?

> His pursuit of happiness paid off because in 2014 Christopher Gardner has a net worth of $60 million. He has helped fund a $50 million project in San Francisco for the creation of low-income housing and opportunities for employment in the area of the city where he was once homeless. The movie earned $163 million in the US and $300 million worldwide, and Will Smith received an Oscar nomination.

1. Can you remember specific times when you said you'd do one thing and then did the exact opposite?
2. How successful have you been at getting the former job related anger and hate out of your mind?

3. What is your plan for your pursuit of
    happiness?

Prayer

Now may the God of hope fill you with all joy and peace in
believing, that you may abound in hope by the power of the
Holy Spirit. Amen. (Romans 15:13)

The Power And Blessing Of Being Together

The power and blessing of faith each person carries with them provide a person with day-by-day direction and a sense of mission in their life, but the power and blessing of being together and sharing faith and mission strengthens each individual's faith limitlessly.

> Again I say to you that if two of you agree on earth concerning anything that they ask, it will be done for them by My Father in heaven. "For where two or more are gathered in My name, I am in the midst of them." (Matthew 18:19-20)

On the morning of September 11, 2001 Yo Yo Ma was in Denver. His wife called shortly after nine o'clock and told him to turn the television on because something bad was happening. When he turned the television on, he saw what was happening in New York and Washington. As he watched, he began to think about his schedule for the few days ahead. He was supposed to do a concert in Colorado Springs on the 11th, another concert in Denver on the 12th, and yet another concert on the 13th in Phoenix. Each concert was with a different major concert orchestra. He knew in the wake of the horrific events of the day each orchestra would have to make a decision about the scheduled concert event.

Amazingly, each orchestra decided they were going to play as scheduled. He was told they may change the program a little, but there would be no other change in the concert event. Each venue director decided it was important to actually be together and have a moment of, literally, of being together. The view was the music would be the way all involved would come together, because all involved were asserting themselves as a community, as a people, as a city, as whatever. On those fateful nights they all needed to be together in the place they had planned to be for the evening. To this day Yo Yo Ma knows he can go back and speak with anyone at one of those concerts in Colorado Springs, Denver or Phoenix after the 9-

11 attacks and know each person will have a vivid memory of what the evening meant not only for them but every other person involved.

On the morning of November 22, 1963 my high school classmates were preparing for a Friday night football game with our crosstown rivals. At the morning pep rally we cheered for victory at the game and celebrated the capture of our crosstown rival's goat mascot. Just after lunch the news of President Kennedy's assassination was broadcast over the network news coming into the TV Journalism classroom and everybody felt a jolt with the news. The school administrators at both my school and the crosstown rival school quickly had to decide whether or not to go ahead with the scheduled football game. The decision was made to go ahead with the game, and it was a good thing because everybody needed to be together after such a horrible day. The game was hard fought, but it ended in a 0-0 tie. It was truly a night to remember, and a night made all the more memorable because rivals had chosen to spend the night together as part of a single community.

For the job seeker participation in one or more job seeker support groups, especially faith-based job seeker support groups, provides not only access to important information on the skills needed for a successful job search but also the power and blessing of being together in His name for a common purpose.

1. Can you remember specific times when you felt the power and blessing of being together in faith?
2. How has being part of a faith-based job seeker support group helped with your job search?
3. Is being part of a faith-based job seeker support group aid you with your job search?
4. What have you done to let other job seekers know about faith-based job seeker support groups?

Prayer

Lord, You said when two or three are gathered together in Your name, then You would be present with them. We pray together in hope of uniting many individual Christians throughout the world who, though separate, are gathered together in another sense to pray to You. Amen.

Who's Minding Your Vineyard?

Jesus presents his teachings very frequently in the form of a parable, which provides a descriptive narrative relating to His teachings. The parables provide a representation of a universal truth by providing a setting, an action and the results of the action. As a simple way of teaching, Jesus was able to convey much of what it meant to be of the "Word". One such parable is the parable of vineyard. The parable tells of a landowner, who planted a vineyard, made many improvements to the vineyard and then left the vineyard on the hands of tenants. The trouble comes when the landowner tries to collect his share of the crop. The first servants he sends to collect the owner's share are beaten, killed or stoned. The same thing happens when he sends another set of servants, and when his son goes to collect the fruit he too is killed. Finally the landowner goes to collect the fruit and Jesus asks what the landowner should do. The disciples think the tenants should be destroyed and the vineyard should be leased to new tenants.

> Jesus said to them, "Have you never read in the scriptures 'The stone which the builders rejected has become the chief cornerstone. This was the Lord's doing, and it is marvelous in our eyes'. "Therefore I say to you, the kingdom of God will be taken from you and given to a nation bearing the fruits of it. And whoever falls on this stone will be broken; but on whomever it falls, it will grind him to powder."
> (Matthew 21:42-44)

The beauty of teaching by the use of parables is each parable can have many meanings and many interpretations with each meaning leading back to the core meaning intended by Jesus.

For example in the parable of the vineyard the landowner could be a job seeker with the vineyard being everything the job seeker does to prepare themselves for their next position, which would include among other things their resume and interview skills practice, and the part of the tenants could be recruiters, headhunters, and perhaps even a few hiring managers the job seeker encounters along the journey between unemployment and full employment.

All too often those recruiters, headhunters, and hiring managers take advantage of the relationship they have with job seekers by using the job seeker to gain additional contacts and leads while leading the job seeker on regarding their prospects for finding employment through them. The leads and contacts the job seeker passes along to the recruiters, headhunters, and hiring managers become the analog for the servants sent by the landowner.

Finally the job seeker fully acknowledges what has happened and moves on and finally achieves their goal of finding new employment while the recruiters, headhunters, and hiring managers are left with nothing as they fall over the fact they lost a candidate, which becomes the cornerstone from the parable.

Even from the perspective of the job seeker the parable of the vineyard is still about how those coming to recognize their sins and come to Christ will be rewarded while those rejecting the Word and living in a disrespectful manner will be punished.

1. Have you ever been in a situation where you felt those tending your vineyard were treating you badly?
2. How did you conclude someone was taking advantage of you in your job search?
3. After a bad experience with a recruiter or headhunter what are you doing differently?
4. What more do you need to better tend your vineyard during the job search?

Prayer

Almighty and everlasting God, you are always more ready to hear than we to pray, and to give more than we either desire or deserve: Pour upon us the abundance of your mercy, forgiving us those things of which our conscience is afraid, and giving us those good things for which we are not worthy to ask, except through the merits and mediation of Jesus Christ our Savior; who lives and reigns with you and the Holy Spirit, one God, for ever and ever. Amen. (Collect: Proper 22-A)

Rejoice In The Lord Always!

St. Paul's Epistle to the Philippians was written while St. Paul was in prison. Even though he was writing while wearing iron handcuffs there is no deep sense he is burdened by his situation. The tone of the Philippians Epistle by Paul is filled with joy with only a hint of sorrow.

> Rejoice in the Lord always; again I will say, rejoice. Let your gentleness be known to all men. The Lord is at hand. Be anxious for nothing, but in everything by prayer and supplication, with thanksgiving, let your requests be made known to God; and the peace of God, which surpasses all understanding, will guard your hearts and minds through Christ Jesus. Finally, brethren, whatever things are true, whatever things are noble, whatever things are just, whatever things are pure, whatever things are lovely, whatever things are of good report, if there is any virtue and if there is anything praiseworthy — meditate on these things. The things which you learned and received and heard and saw in me, these do, the God of peace will be with you. (Philippians 4:4-9)

Hardly the words someone might expect to be coming from a man sitting in a prison cell while his hands are bound by iron cuffs.

The journey of a job seeker can be likened to the journey followed by many early Christian disciples, including St. Paul. Each such journey included its successes and disappointments. St. Paul reminds himself and anyone listening to remember the importance of prayer as a part of any journey.

The job seeker wants to be victorious in their job search, but St. Paul reminds the job seeker to always rejoice in the Lord and keep prayer as the essential ingredient for attaining victory over worry along every part of the journey.

St. Paul reminds the job seeker to keep prayer a part of everything, and each prayer must include both supplication and thanksgiving.

Supplication is necessary in prayer to provide focus and to ensure God knows the job seeker is asking specifically for help.

Thanksgiving is necessary in prayer as a sign of humility to ensure God knows the job seeker will be content and thankful for whatever God wisely and lovingly provides.

When the job seeker frames their requests in the devotion of a prayer including specific requests for help and with a thankful heart for everything God designs for the job seeker, including both the pleasures and the pain, the job seeker can take comfort knowing peace will guard their mind and free them of anxiety in a way defying mere rational explanation. In short, the act of rejoicing through such prayer devotion will surpass all understanding.

1. How often have you taken the time to simply rejoice in the Lord?
2. Is prayerful devotion an essential part of your job search?
3. When you pray do you include both specific requests for help and thanks for whatever God provides?
4. What steps can you take to make rejoicing in the Lord a more frequent part of your job search?

Prayer
Lord, we pray that your grace may always precede and follow us, that we may continually be given to good works; through Jesus Christ our Lord, who lives and reigns with you and the Holy Spirit, one God, now and for ever. Amen.
(Collect: Proper 23-A)

Whose Job Search Is It Anyway?

From the perspective of the Pharisees Jesus was both a religious and political threat. Jesus was perceived as so much of a threat the Pharisees teamed up with the Herodians, whom they hated. The Pharisees had to trap Jesus in such a way there would be no way out for him either with the Jews or with the Roman occupiers. The Pharisees thought they had devised the perfect plan to trap Jesus.

> The Pharisees went and plotted to entrap Jesus in what he said. So they sent their disciples to him, along with the Herodians, saying, "Teacher, we know that you are sincere, and teach the way of God in accordance with truth, and show deference to no one; for you do not regard people with partiality. Tell us, then, what you think. Is it lawful to pay taxes to the emperor, or not?" But Jesus, aware of their malice, said, "Why are you putting me to the test, you hypocrites? Show me the coin used for the tax." And they brought him a denarius. Then he said to them, "Whose head is this, and whose title?" They answered, "The emperor's." Then he said to them, "Give therefore to the emperor the things that are the emperor's, and to God the things that are God's." When they heard this, they were amazed; and they left him and went away. (Matthew 22:15-22)

The Pharisees made a monumental mistake. They thought Jesus wanted to be King of Israel and was simply the son of Joseph and Mary. The Pharisees thought the influence of Jesus would end with his death on the cross.

In the end what was supposed to be a foolproof trap provides the prompt for one of Jesus' greatest teachings. Jesus' response to the question may seem simple and straight forward, but the implications of the response have echoed through two millennia and shaped western societies.

The question is just as timely today as it was at the very beginning of the first millennium. The question is appropriate when asking about things well beyond coinage, including the very motives driving people through the course of each day.

Indeed, the question applies even to how a job seeker proceeds through the course of their job search. At each step along the journey the job seeker must consciously make a decision to follow the path of "Caesar" leading away from God's intended path or follow the path set down by the Lord leading to a destination by the most direct route.

Each day when the job seeker awakens they begin making choices in the form of decisions regarding what to render to "Caesar" and what to render to God. With each decision throughout each day the job seeker runs the risk of being blinded like the Pharisees, who were on the wrong side of history, even though the Lord may be sending signals constantly. The job seeker must be careful all along the way to follow the direction leading to what will become the completion of their mission in life.

1. In a job search how does the job seeker know what is Caesar's and what is the Lord's?
2. What could push a job seeker to the wrong path during a job search?
3. When you stray towards the path away for the Lord how do you make the course correction?
4. Have you ever taken the time to help others regain their footing on the right path?

Prayer
Almighty and everlasting God, in Christ you have revealed your glory among the nations: Preserve the works of your mercy, that your Church throughout the world may persevere with steadfast faith in the confession of your Name; through Jesus Christ our Lord, who lives and reigns with you and the Holy Spirit, one God, for ever and ever. Amen.
(Collect: Proper 24-A)

Doing What Matters Most

Jesus faced many challenges from the various elite sects of the Jewish community. None of the encounters provides a better example regarding the issue of what matters most in the lives of the faithful than Jesus' encounter with the Pharisees in the Gospel of Matthew.

> When the Pharisees heard that Jesus had silenced the Sadducees, they gathered together, and one of them, a lawyer, asked him a question to test him. "Teacher, which commandment in the law is the greatest?" He said to him, "`You shall love the Lord your God with all your heart, and with all your soul, and with all your mind.' This is the greatest and first commandment. And a second is like it: `You shall love your neighbor as yourself.' On these two commandments hang all the law and the prophets." (Matthew 22:34-40)

> You shall have no other gods before Me. (Exodus 20:3)

> You shall not bear false witness against your neighbor. (Exodus 20:16)

The importance and value of Jesus' answer remains true in both the best of times and the worst of times. The answer is just as true today as it was at the beginning of the first millennia or at any other point in history during the Christian Era.

The true meaning of the first part of Jesus' answer goes well beyond the mere notion of worshiping other gods but also anything a person might put in place of a god whether it is demon, power, money, pleasure, drug, nation, or political belief. Indeed, any form of idolatry becomes a violation of the first commandment.

The second part of Jesus' answer should be clear. You are supposed to love your neighbor as yourself. Or, in other words, neighbors should always receive the best from those they encounter rather than just what is convenient or easy to provide.

There is no special dispensation given to someone just because they are a job seeker or even when they are engaged in helping job seekers. A part of a job seeker's or job seeker coach's role is to provide the very best they have when helping a job seeker. There should be no pause or hesitation in stepping up to offer the best because the best is what anybody expects. In other words, cutting corners or giving just enough to get by is going to be good enough. Offering less than the best cheats everybody, and is clearly not what Jesus intended.

1. Do you have more trouble with the first or second part of Jesus' answer to the Pharisees?
2. What types of distractions cloud your ability to put God first in your life?
3. Are you giving your best when helping others with their job search?
4. Would you be satisfied being your own neighbor?
5. What can you do to better live by Jesus' answer to the Pharisees?

Prayer
Hear our prayers, O Lord, and consider our desires. Give unto us true humility, a meek and quiet spirit, a loving and a friendly, a holy and a useful manner of life; bearing the burdens of our neighbors, denying ourselves, and studying to benefit others, and to please Thee in all things. Grant us to be righteous in performing promises, loving to our relatives, careful of our charges, slow to anger, and readily prepared for every good work. Amen. Jeremy Taylor (1613-1667)

Before The Throne In White Robes

The Book of Revelation was authored by John of Patmos, who is also known as John the Divine. Of all the visions presented in the Book of Revelation none is more striking and relevant than the vision most commonly referenced on All Saints Day.

> After these things I looked, and behold, a great multitude which no one could number, of all nations, tribes, peoples, and tongues, standing before the throne and before the Lamb, clothed with white robes, with palm branches in their hands, and crying out with a loud voice, saying, Salvation belongs to our God who sits on the throne, and to the Lamb!" All the angels stood around the throne and the elders and the four living creatures, and fell on their faces before the throne and worshiped God, saying: "Amen! Blessing and glory and wisdom, Thanksgiving and honor and power and might, Be to our God forever and ever. Amen." Then one of the elders answer, saying to me, "Who are these arrayed in white robes, and where did they come from?" And I said to him, "Sir, you know." So he said to me, "These are the ones who come out of the great tribulation, and washed their robes and made them white in the blood of the Lamb. "Therefore they are before the throne of God, and serve Him day and night in His temple. And He who sits on the throne will dwell among them. They shall neither hunger anymore nor thirst anymore; the sun shall not strike them, nor any heat; for the Lamb who is in the midst of the throne will shepherd them and lead them to living fountains of waters. And God will wipe away every tear from their eyes." (Revelation 7:9-17)

In the early days of the Christian Church those clothed with white robes were thought to include Christian martyrs, but more recently the view includes anybody having gone through a great tribulation, which today would include almost any faithful Christian.

Certainly the definition of "great tribulation" would include those having experienced natural disaster, war, a life of disability, economic collapse, and any other calamity. There has certainly been enough tribulation to go around during the past couple millennia to touch everybody.

Those throughout time experiencing the tribulation of an extended period of unemployment surely qualify as having been through a great tribulation, and are surely worthy through their faith in having the robes made white in the blood of the Lamb, which is the forgiveness all of the faithful receive from Jesus' sacrifice on the cross.

1. How does your faith bring you comfort during a time of tribulation?
2. Can you envision yourself around the throne of God?
3. Does your faith make your time of tribulation easier to bear?
4. Have you ever been able to help someone come to accept their special place around God's throne?

Prayer

How shining and splendid are your gifts, O Lord which you
give us for our eternal well-being Your glory shines radiantly in
your saints, O God In the honor and noble victory of the
martyrs. The white-robed company follow you, bright with
their abundant faith; They scorned the wicked words of those
with this world's power. For you they sustained fierce
beatings, chains, and torments, they were drained by cruel
punishments. They bore their holy witness to you who were
grounded deep within their hearts; they were sustained by
patience and constancy. Endowed with your everlasting grace,
may we rejoice forever with the martyrs in our bright
fatherland. O Christ, in your goodness, grant to us the gracious
heavenly realms of eternal life. Amen.

(Unknown author, 10th century)

Keeping The Lamps Burning

Of all of Jesus' parables the parable of the ten bridesmaids provides the most lessons for job seekers both in symbolism and substance. The parable is meant to serve as a reminder for being prepared for the second coming, but for the job seeker being prepared for the new job is also very important.

Jesus said, "Then the kingdom of heaven will be like this. Ten bridesmaids took their lamps and went to meet the bridegroom. Five of them were foolish, and five were wise. When the foolish took their lamps, they took no oil with them; but the wise took flasks of oil with their lamps. As the bridegroom was delayed, all of them became drowsy and slept. But at midnight there was a shout, `Look! Here is the bridegroom! Come out to meet him.' Then all those bridesmaids got up and trimmed their lamps. The foolish said to the wise, `Give us some of your oil, for our lamps are going out.' But the wise replied, `No! there will not be enough for you and for us; you had better go to the dealers and buy some for yourselves.' And while they went to buy it, the bridegroom came, and those who were ready went with him into the wedding banquet; and the door was shut. Later the other bridesmaids came also, saying, `Lord, lord, open to us.' But he replied, `Truly I tell you, I do not know you.' Keep awake therefore, for you know neither the day nor the hour."
(Matthew 25:1-13)

In the time of Jesus weddings were scheduled most often during at the end of harvest season, and it was never known at exactly at what hour the groom would arrive at the bride's home and escort her to the wedding banquet, which meant the bridesmaids' role was to provide light for the wedding procession to the wedding banquet. In the parable Jesus is the groom and the Church is the bride.

For job seekers each element in the parable provides an analog and a valuable lesson. For a job seeker the groom is the new job while the job seeker's family/loved ones are the bride. The job seeker is one of the bridesmaids. The oil becomes the resources the job seeker has gathered, the wick becomes the ability to use the resources to produce light, and the lamp light becomes the job seeker's ability to navigate the job search path with confidence and faith.

When the job seeker has gathered not only the resources but also the knowledge to use the resources they will be successful in their job search. When the job seeker has not gathered sufficient resources and knowledge their job search journey will not end successfully, and they will see only a shut door. In addition, the unprepared job seeker cannot expect much in the way of last minute help from those they might be competing against in the job search because those other job seekers must ensure their own success in the job search.

1. Are you prepared for the job search or not prepared for the job search?
2. Do you need more job search resources or more knowledge in how to use the job search resources?
3. Are you prepared for any delays along the job search journey?
4. Would you fault a job seeker competing against you when they think first about themselves?

Prayer

Be pleased, O God, to deliver me; O LORD, make haste to help me. Let those who seek my life be ashamed and altogether dismayed; let those who take pleasure in my misfortune draw back and be disgraced. Let those who say to me "Aha!" and gloat over me turn back, because they are ashamed. Let all who seek you rejoice and be glad in you; let those who love your salvation say for ever, "Great is the LORD!" But as for me, I am poor and needy; come to me speedily, O God. You are my helper and my deliverer; O LORD, do not tarry. Amen. (Psalm 70)

Oh Thank Edmund

Edmund the Martyr, who is also known as St. Edmund or Edmund of East Anglia, died November 20, 869. Edmund of East Anglia was king of East Anglia from about 855 until his death. Edmund of East Anglia became a martyr as the result of an invasion by the Great Heathen Army, which were previously uncoordinated bands of Vikings from Sweden, Norway, and Denmark. The invaders demanded Edmund of East Anglia to renounce Christ, but he refused. Instead he disbanded his army to avoid a massacre, but he was caught, tortured, and killed by the invaders while calling upon Jesus. The designated Gospel for Edmund the Martyr's feast day is as follows:

> Jesus said to the twelve apostles, "See, I am sending you out like sheep into the midst of wolves; so be wise as serpents and innocent as doves. Beware of them, for they will hand you over to councils and flog you in their synagogues; and you will be dragged before governors and kings because of me, as a testimony to them and the Gentiles. When they hand you over, do not worry about how you are to speak or what you are to say; for what you are to say will be given to you at that time; for it is not you who speak, but the Spirit of your Father speaking through you. Brother will betray brother to death, and a father his child, and children will rise against parents and have them put to death; and you will be hated by all because of my name. But the one who endures to the end will be saved." (Matthew 10:16-22)

St. Edmund is the patron saint of pandemics because pandemics attack a population much as the Great Heathen Army attacked villages and towns in the 9th century. St. Edmund is also the patron saint of kings because in wanting to spare his kingdom from a massacre while standing true to his faith he set an example, which has become the embodiment of a king's claims to divinely-ordained rule, rightful sovereignty and the binding links between king, land and society.

For job seekers each new day presents a reminder of just how tough it is to be sent out like a sheep into the midst of wolves, and each day the job seeker must remember the Holy Spirit is with them throughout the day. The job search journey is never truly easy, but it becomes a whole lot more bearable knowing Christ has prepared the way and will be there all along the route.

Having faith makes the job search journey easier, but being prepared with knowledge of the road ahead and what must be done at each step along the route makes the journey sure and true to its destination. Having the strength of faith, as did Edmund the Martyr, enables the job seeker to let the Spirit of the Father speak through them.

1. As a job seeker, do you frequently feel like a sheep being let out to wolves?
2. Has a fear of being amongst the wolves ever kept you from stepping into the fray?
3. Have you ever felt the Spirit of the Father guiding you in speech or actions as a job seeker?
4. What would you say to another job seeker facing a fear of being amongst the wolves?

Prayer
O God of ineffable mercy, you gave grace and fortitude to blessed Edmund the king to triumph over the enemy of his people by nobly dying for your Name: Bestow on us your servants the shield of faith with which we can withstand the assaults of our ancient enemy; through Jesus Christ our Redeemer, who lives and reigns with you and the Holy Spirit, one God, now and for ever. Amen.

Thank God Always

The simplest prayer any faithful person can give at the start each day is to say, "Thank you". Regardless of a person's individual circumstance there is always much to be thankful for at the beginning of each day because to all much is given. Perhaps no scripture does a better job of expressing the spirit of thanks giving as well as the opening verses of 1 Corinthians.

> Grace to you and peace from God our Father and the Lord Jesus Christ. I thank my God always concerning you for the grace of God which was given to you by Christ Jesus, that you were enriched in everything by Him in all utterance and all knowledge, even as the testimony of Christ was confirmed in you, so that you come short in no gift, eagerly waiting for the revelation of our Lord Jesus Christ, who will also confirm you to the end, that you may be blameless in the day of our Lord Jesus Christ. God is faithful, by whom you were called into the fellowship of His Son, Jesus Christ our Lord. (1 Corinthians 1:3-9)

Regardless of a person's station in life or their individual immediate situation the passage from St. Paul's first letter to the Corinthians states the individual will have tremendous stability when they let their faith define who they are in relation to God rather than letting the world define who they are in relation to things, groups and circumstances.

Indeed, the defining strength of faith realized by truly acknowledging where a person stands in relation to God provides a shield of protection against the world's attempts to leverage an individual's resolve and faith by means of defining them in terms of secular things the individual may not have in their possession. With the shield of faith the individual will not crumple with insecurity, dissatisfaction and covetousness, but will stand like as an independent free agent knowing who they really are and what their life really means in relation to God.

For the job seeker there is a special need to remember the prayer of thanks each day coupled with the need to always remember to define themselves based on their special relationship with God because in doing so they reinforce the truth related to what God has already given to them as they begin their day.

When the job seeker fully accepts the fact God will short them no gift and will confirm them to the end they are much better prepared to face all of the secular barriers they may confront along the path of the job search journey.

1. How often do you give thanks to God for the gifts you have already received from Him?
2. Do you find strength in defining yourself based on your faith as you face a secular world?
3. Are you ready to face the attempts to crumple you with insecurity, dissatisfaction and covetousness?
4. What can you do to share your faith in ways to support others needing encouragement with their faith?

Prayer
Almighty God, give us grace to cast away the works of darkness, and put on the armor of light, now in the time of this mortal life in which your Son Jesus Christ came to visit us in great humility; that in the last day, when he shall come again in his glorious majesty to judge both the living and the dead, we may rise to the life immortal; through him who lives and reigns with you and the Holy Spirit, one God, now and for ever. Amen. (Advent 1 Collect)

Let Your Light Shine Before Others

The mark of true devotion in Christianity is in sharing faith openly and plainly in front of the whole world. True disciples happily preach the Gospel and allow the Lord's righteousness to shine out through them. True faith cannot hide the joy and love for Christ any better than a football fan can hide their love of their team or a mother can hide her love for her children. When the Light of Life truly comes from within someone, it will not remain hidden. The light will always be visible to the outside world.

Jesus said, "You are the salt of the earth; but if salt has lost its taste, how can its saltiness be restored? It is no longer good for anything, but is thrown out and trampled under foot. "You are the light of the world. A city built on a hill cannot be hid. No one after lighting a lamp puts it under the bushel basket, but on the lampstand, and it gives light to all in the house. In the same way, let your light shine before others, so that they may see your good works and give glory to your Father in heaven. "Do not think that I have come to abolish the law or the prophets; I have come not to abolish but to fulfill. For truly I tell you, until heaven and earth pass away, not one letter, not one stroke of a letter, will pass from the law until all is accomplished. Therefore, whoever breaks one of the least of these commandments, and teaches others to do the same, will be called least in the kingdom of heaven; but whoever does them and teaches them will be called great in the kingdom of heaven." (Matthew 5:13-19)

When someone takes a light into a darkened room it will illuminate the room according to its strength. And even a dim light is better than a burned out or a covered light bulb.

Job seekers must let their light shine from the best spot to ensure the light has the most reach. If a job seeker does not shine their light, no one will. If job seekers do not constantly strive to spread the word of their skills and experience, no one will know of their strengths. Nobody can be expected to spread the word for a job seeker without the job seeker's initial energy and effort to shine on their own.

Just as Christians are the means by which Jesus is revealed in world today a job seeker must use the faith they have in themselves to provide the means by which potential employers will know them. Just as the faithful are the hands and feet by which the words of Scripture move from the Bible into everyday life the job seeker must use their hands and feet to get the word of their skills, experience and accomplishments before the eyes and ears of potential employers.

1. Is your inner light bright enough to illuminate your journey through your job search?
2. Do you have difficulty positioning your light in a way to illuminate the way to interviews and offers?
3. Do you have difficulty finding the fuel to keep your job search light shining brightly?
4. What do you need to make your job search light burn even more brightly in the days ahead?

Prayer
This little light of mine, I'm gonna let it shine. This little light of mine, I'm gonna let it shine Let it shine, let it shine, let it shine. Won't let Satan blow it out. I'm gonna let it shine. Won't let Satan blow it out. I'm gonna let it shine, let it shine, let it shine, let it shine. Let it shine til Jesus comes. I'm gonna let it shine. Let it shine til Jesus comes. I'm gonna let it shine, let it shine, let it shine, let it shine. Hide it under a bushel, no! I'm gonna let it shine. Hide it under a bushel, no! I'm gonna let it shine, Let it shine, let it shine, let it shine. Amen.
(Lyrics: "This Little Light Of Mine")

On Getting Directions And Getting Away From The Dock

The story of the wise men making the journey to meet the Christ child and present Him with gifts is truly iconic. The fact they had traveled a great distance just to bring gifts provides a wonderful image of the season, but it turns out one of the most important parts of the story is what they finally had to do to complete their journey. They were guys, and, unlike most guys, they actually stopped to get directions.

> Now after Jesus was born in Bethlehem of Judea in the days of Herod the king, behold, wise men from the East came to Jerusalem saying, Where is He who has been born King of the Jews? For we have seen His star in the East and have come to worship Him. When Herod the king heard this, he was troubled, and all Jerusalem with him. And when he had gathered all the chief priests and scribes of the people together, he inquired of them where the Christ was to be born. So they said to him, "In Bethlehem of Judea, for thus it is written by the prophet: "But you, Bethlehem, in the land of Judah, are not the least among the rulers of Judah; for out of you shall come a Ruler who will shepherd My people of Israel". The Herod, when he had secretly called the wise men, determined from them what time the star appeared. And he sent them to Bethlehem and said, "Go and search carefully for the young Child, and when you have found Him, bring back word to me, that I may come and worship Him also. When they heard the king, they departed; and behold, the star which they had seen in the East went before them, till it came and stood over where the young Child was. When they saw the star, they rejoiced with exceedingly great joy. (Matthew 2:1-10)

Of course, the wise men found the Christ child, presented their three gifts in the form of gold, frankincense and myrrh, and returned home without seeing Herod again. Had the wise men not found the Christ child Epiphany would be something completely different. Had the wise men not even bothered to follow the star with the goal of presenting gifts for the Christ child much of the tradition surrounding the birth of Jesus would be different.

Fortunately, the wise men did the unexpected for men and actually asked for directions, and then they were able to follow the directions successfully to reach their intended destination, and, as a result, there was an Epiphany. Perhaps they asked for directions because they were from the East.

Had the wise men stayed longer they may have also eventually said, "Sometimes people in the west remind me of people sitting in a rowboat. With great sincerity and earnestness they row and row while refusing to untie the boat from the dock."

Of all the things a job seeker must remember on an ongoing basis two of the most important things to remember are to always be ready to ask for directions and always check to ensure they untied the boat from the dock.

1. When was the last time you asked for directions regarding your job search?
2. If you have recently asked for such directions, are you sure you asked the right questions?
3. Have you ever felt like you were rowing and rowing and not getting anywhere?
4. What do you need to ensure you get the right directions and have untied from the dock?

Prayer
O God, by the leading of a star you manifested your only Son to the peoples of the earth: Lead us, who know you now by faith, to your presence, where we may see your glory face to face; through Jesus Christ our Lord, who lives and reigns with you and the Holy Spirit, one God, now and for ever. Amen. (Epiphany Collect)

Fear Makes the Wolf Bigger Than He Is

Emotions are powerful. Emotions can either be helpful or harmful. If someone allows fear to take over, they are in real trouble. The Bible includes many passages where fear and overcoming fear become a key part of the message.

Peace I leave you. My peace I give you; not as the world gives do I give to you. Let not your heart be troubled, neither let it be afraid. (John 14:27)

And David said to his son Solomon. "Be strong and of good courage, and do it; do not fear nor be dismayed, for the Lord God — my God — will be with you. He will not leave you nor forsake you, until you have finished all the work for the service of the house of the Lord." (1 Chronicles 28:20)

Fear not, for I am with you; Be not dismayed, for I am your God. I will strengthen you, Yes, I will help you, I will uphold you with My righteous right hand. (Isaiah 41:10)

Yea, though I walk through the valley of the shadow of death, I will fear no evil; For You are with me; Your rod and Your staff, they comfort me. (Psalm 23:4)

A German proverb reminds everybody "Fear makes the wolf bigger than he is". It is normal for everyone to face many things in life causing concern. Adding fear to the mix with the concerns causes trouble to be magnified many times with the result being a situation the individual might not be able to handle.

When someone feels fear, they must make a choice. Either they continue to live in terror or they face their fear and do what needs to be done anyway. Being of resolute mind is one way to push past fear, but it always feels better to have the knowledge God is present and ready to help.

When President Franklin D. Roosevelt delivered his first Inaugural Address on March 4, 1933 the entire world was languishing in the deepest part of the Great Depression. At the time of his first inauguration a quarter of the workforce was unemployed, and the Country was in the middle of a bank panic. With such a backdrop President Roosevelt's Inaugural Address included the now famous quote as follows:

> So, first of all, let me assert my firm belief that the only thing we have to fear is fear itself — nameless, unreasoning, unjustified terror which paralyzes needed efforts to convert retreat into advance.

The very next day President Roosevelt declared a "bank holiday" and a special session of Congress was convened on March 9, which passed the Emergency Banking Act.

The job seeker must be particularly mindful and resolute concerning their fears because otherwise their troubles will surely be magnified many times.

1. What do you most fear regarding your current time between jobs and your job search?
2. What gives you the most trouble when trying to overcome your fears?
3. What, if anything, provides you with relief from your job search related fears?
4. What, short of a job offer, do you most need to overcome fear related to your job search?

Prayer
Dear gracious Lord, thank You that we can depend on You. We take refuge in You every day in this our time of need. Thank You for giving us freedom from every fear. Through Jesus Christ our Lord, who with you and the Holy Spirit lives and reigns, one God, now and for ever. Amen.

Let's Play Two!

In times of trouble, loss and despair even the faithful may begin to wonder whether or not God is with them and acting to guide them. It is at such times people must remember the word of God presented in the Bible is a message of joy and good for the faithful. At the outset of His mission Jesus proclaimed the good news of God as a key part of His disciple recruitment.

> Now after John was arrested, Jesus came to Galilee, proclaiming the good news of God, and saying, "The time is fulfilled, and the kingdom of God has come near; repent, and believe in the good news."
> (Mark 1:14-15)

Each of the Apostles proclaimed the good news as they went forth in His name, and the Apostle Paul became the most prolific at delivering the message.

> Rejoice in the Lord always. Again I will say, rejoice! Let your gentleness be known to all men. The Lord is at hand. Be anxious for nothing, but in everything by prayer and supplication, with thanksgiving, let your requests be made known to God; and the peace of God, which surpasses all understanding, will guard your hearts and minds through Christ Jesus.
> (Philippians 4:4-7)

In short, the good news is with the faithful always, which means they should always be of good cheer by simply knowing God is with them.

Ernie Banks played with the Chicago Cubs for nineteen (19) seasons and became known as "Mr. Cub". Banks was the first African-American signed to play with the Chicago Cubs, and he spent his entire Major League Baseball career with the Chicago Cubs while never playing in a single post-season game. He was a symbol of the joyful abandon the game of baseball brings to players and fans alike. Ernie Banks' favorite line was always:

"It's a great day for a ball game; let's play two."

Ernie Banks is a baseball icon whose eternal optimism and zest for life was always reflected in his smile. Upon hitting his 500th home run Ernie Banks said:

"The riches of the game are in the thrills, not the money."

By example and his own energy Ernie Banks showed a generation of baseball fans along with anybody else caring to look for a way to enjoy life and be happy. Regarding happiness Ernie Banks said:

"You must try to generate happiness within yourself. If you aren't happy in one place, chances are you won't be happy anyplace."

Job seekers should think about the Chicago Cubs and Ernie Banks as they move through their time as a job seeker because even though Ernie Banks never played in a post-season game and the Chicago Cubs haven't won a World Series since 1908 there is still a tremendous amount of pride, joyfulness, spirit, and hope voiced by every Chicago Cubs player and fan year after year. So the next time a job seeker is feeling a little sad, they should remember Ernie Banks and say:

"It's a great day for a ball game; let's play two".

1. What makes you smile when you begin each day during your job search?
2. Do you take a moment in each day to count your blessings and reasons why you can smile?
3. What do you do when you begin to feel anxious about your job search?

4. How does the role of those around you help or hinder your job search?

Prayer

Give us grace, O Lord, to answer readily the call of our Savior Jesus Christ and proclaim to all people the Good News of His salvation, that we and the whole world may perceive the glory of His marvelous works; who lives and reigns with you and the Holy Spirit, one God, for ever and ever. Amen.

Show Up!

The Bible would be a forgotten book had it not been for the fact the faithful not only heard the word of God but also wanted to share the word of God with others. In other words, they had to not only hold their faith but also "show up" as an active messenger in the work of passing along the word of God to others.

> And let us not grow weary while doing good, for in due season we shall reap if we do not lose heart.
> (Galatians 6:9)

> Then He spoke a parable to them, that men always ought to pray and not lose heart, saying: "There was in a certain city a judge who did not fear God nor regard man. Now there was a widow in that city; and she came to him, saying, 'Get justice for me from my adversary.' And he would not for a while; but afterward he said within himself, 'Though I do not fear God nor regard man, yet because this widow troubles me I will avenge her, lest by her continual coming she weary me.'" (Luke 18:1-5)

> Therefore my beloved brethren, be steadfast, immovable, always abounding in the work of the Lord, knowing that your labor is not in vain in the Lord.
> (1 Corinthians 15:58)

> But as for you, brethren, do not grow weary in doing good. (2 Thessalonians 3:13)

> The soul of a lazy man desires, and has nothing; but the soul of the diligent shall be made rich.
> (Proverbs 13:4)

In short, anything truly worth achieving should be worth working to achieve, and the first step to working towards a goal is to show up not only with steadfast desire to achieve the goal but also a plan for getting to the goal.

Achieving success as a job seeker is no different than achieving success at any other endeavor. Perhaps the main difference between achieving success as a job seeker and achieving success while employed is in the nature of the work environment and structure, which makes it all the more important for the job seeker to always show up ready to accomplish the task at hand.

1. What about showing up is difficult for you during your job search?
2. What do you do on a daily basis to ensure you show up for your job search?
3. How do you remind yourself to stay persistent with your job search by showing up every day?
4. What do you need to make it easier to ensure you show up every day for your job search?

Prayer
Give us grace, O Lord, to be steadfast and always ready to show up for the work ahead in our job search. Give us the strength of persistence to show up each and every day as we work through the job search process as we move toward the time when we have fully secured our new employment. Through Jesus Christ our Lord, who with you and the Holy Spirit lives and reigns, one God, now and for ever. Amen.

Step By Step

During the early days of Jesus' mission He had to not only firmly establish His goals for Himself and His disciples but also solidify His plan to spread His teachings across the land both while His disciples were with Him and for the time when His disciples would be on their own.

> Now in the morning, having risen a long while before daylight He went out and departed to a solitary place; and there He prayed. And Simon and those who were with Him searched for Him. When they found Him, they said to Him, "Everyone is looking for You." But He said to them, "Let us go into the next towns, that I may preach there also, because for this purpose I have come forth." And He was preaching in their synagogues throughout all Galilee, and casting out demons. (Mark 1:35-39)

The passage at the opening of the Gospel of Mark clearly illustrates how Jesus knew His mission and had set out to get to His goal in a step by step manner by going to synagogue after synagogue throughout Galilee, and all along the way he would be not only preaching His message but also casting out demons. By setting the example He showed His disciples how to spread His message through the lands not only in the short run but also throughout history.

Five hundred years before the Christian Era Lao Tzu, who was a Chinese Zhou Dynasty philosopher, wrote the "Tao Te Ching". The "Tao Te Ching" title can be translated to "The Classic/Canon of the Way/Path and the Power/Virtue." The quotation most well known from the "Tao Te Ching" states, "A journey of a thousand miles begins with a single step." Perhaps the second most familiar quotation from the work states, "He who knows others is wise; He who know himself is enlightened." Together the two quotations convey essentially the same meaning as the passage from Gospel of Mark.

Setting goals, establishing plans and the step by step execution of those plans are essential for success in any endeavor.

Our goals can only be reached through a vehicle of a plan, in which we must fervently believe, and upon which we must vigorously act. There is no other route to success. (Pablo Picasso)

A good plan violently executed now is better than a perfect plan executed next week. (George S. Patton)

To ensure success a job seeker must not only be both "wise" and "enlightened" but also have a plan to get to their goal in a step by step course. Along the way the job seeker is sure to encounter some demons to be vanquished, and some of those demons will come from within them.

1. Are you at the setting goals level, planning level or step by step execution of a plan level?
2. What have you done to progress from goal setting to planning to plan execution?
3. What demons have you encountered along your job search journey?
4. What do you need to ensure you get to and through the step by step execution of a plan?

Prayer
Lord, grant us strength as we establish our goals, build our plan and navigate our way step by step as we move towards our next opportunity. Provide us with the wisdom to meet many able to guide us along our journey while also granting us the enlightenment to know ourselves. Help us to vanquish the demons we face along our journey both as we encounter them along the way but also as we encounter them within ourselves. Through Jesus Christ our Lord, who with you and the Holy Spirit lives and reigns, one God, now and for ever. Amen.

Apply The Shine

The Transfiguration of Jesus provides a pivotal moment for Jesus and his presence amongst us. For many Christians the Transfiguration of Jesus is viewed as a preview and anticipation of the Resurrection. Indeed, the glory of the Transfiguration, and the cautionary message of Jesus, can only best be understood in the context of His death and resurrection, and not simply on its own.

> Now after six days Jesus took Peter, James, and John, and led them up on a high mountain apart by themselves; and He was transfigured before them. His clothes became shining, exceedingly white, like snow, such as no launderer on earth can whiten them.
> (Mark 9:2-3)

The Transfiguration solidifies the connection between Jesus the man and Jesus the "Son of God", and it provides all the more reason for the disciples to listen to His teachings. Put simply the Transfiguration is an essential step Jesus had to complete on His path between His birth, death on the cross and Resurrection.

All job seekers regardless of where they had been or what they had been doing prior to starting their job search are in a state of transition. Perhaps the most significant event for any job seeker is the moment they discover and accept the fact their job search journey must include a transfiguration because without knowing and accepting the fact they must complete their own personal transfiguration the job search journey never truly begins.

When the job seeker begins their job search they may say to themselves or hear such things as "you need to polish up your resume", "you need to polish up on your interviewing skills", or "you need to polish up on your networking skills". The "polish up" phrase may be applied to other activities, but in each case the call to action relates to something the job seeker must do to transfigure themselves into the "ideal job seeker".

With each application of polish a job seeker applies to the job search the brighter the shine they will have when viewed by potential employers and those others in a position to connect them with employers. Each day the job seeker needs to apply just a little more shine with the knowledge each bit of polish will move the job seeker a bit closer to their final destination of being fully employed.

Also the job seeker must constantly be on the lookout for new ways to "polish up" their skills to ensure no path is ignored along the job search journey.

1. What have you done or what are you doing to apply a brighter shine for your job search experience?
2. What parts of the "polish up" process are giving you the most trouble?
3. How much of your time is spent on actively applying a brighter shine for your job search experience?
4. What do you most need to ensure you are getting the right tools for your "polish up" activities?

Prayer
Lord, help us move ever forward in our quest to improve our job search skills to ensure we obtain not only the basic skills necessary to shorten our job search journey but also the strength to apply our new skills in ways leading most directly to our goal of full employment. Let us not miss those opportunities to build upon our skills simply because we meet with an unexpected challenge. Guide us in the discovery of how our transfigured self can be a blessing for our future employer. Through Jesus Christ our Lord, who with you and the Holy Spirit lives and reigns, one God, now and for ever. Amen.

Thread The Needle

One very memorable statement in the canonical gospels of Matthew, Mark and Luke Jesus describes just how difficult it might be for a rich man to enter the kingdom of God. The Gospel of Luke provides the most detailed information on the issue.

> He said, "How hard is it for those who have riches to enter the kingdom of God! For it is easier for a camel to go through the eye of a needle than for a rich man to enter the kingdom of God." And those who heard it said, "Who then can be saved?" But He said, "The things which are impossible with men are possible with God." (Luke 18:24-27)

The statement regarding the camel and the eye of the needle is one of the places where Jesus intended no metaphor. Jesus quite literally meant exactly what He said. Indeed, Jesus spoke more than once about what was required for entry into the kingdom of God, and neither wealth nor mere good religious habits provide a clear path into the kingdom of God.

Job seekers frequently pose a very similar question along their job search journey. All too often a job seeker asks, "What do I do when someone tells me I am overqualified for a position?" In such a situation the job seeker is saying somebody thinks they are "too rich" for the position. At such times many job seekers fall into a state of job search paralysis thinking all is lost because they seem to be "overqualified" for every position they find or identify.

At such times the job seeker needs to sit back and rethink not only how they might handle the situation in an interview situation but also how to better select their choices regarding what positions they should be sending in an application. Perhaps the job seeker's selection process can be made easier by better presenting themselves through their resume or in the phone interview, but when a job seeker encounters such situations they definitely need to review their choices.

As much as anything, the job seeker needs to remember the last sentence of the passage from Luke where Jesus states, "The things which are impossible with men are possible with God." In short, everybody needs the help of the Lord to gain entry to the kingdom of God, and every job seeker needs to remember to let the Lord be with them all along their job search journey.

Job seekers also need to remember the job search process is very much a matter of threading the needle between what is possible and what the job seeker would like to achieve in the job search. Finally, the job seeker must hold the faith to accept the Lord's pronouncement regarding what is impossible with men is possible with God.

1. How are you handling what to say when someone says you are overqualified?
2. Are you applying for positions where being overqualified is not an issue?
3. How do you match your resume and interview responses to your job applications?
4. What do you most need to ensure you are threading the needle when applying for a position?

Prayer

Lord, grant us the wisdom to thread the needle between what is possible and what we want to achieve not only in our job search but also in our daily interaction with others both at home and beyond the home. Dear Lord provide us with a discerning heart enabling us to find joy and comfort in the midst of our time as a job seeker. Lord enable us to appreciate what joy and solace we find in our time as job seeker to ensure we don't fail to see and grasp what opportunities presented to us. Through Jesus Christ our Lord, who with you and the Holy Spirit lives and reigns, one God, now and for ever. Amen.

The Obstacle Is Not The Road

As Jesus moved along His road of life from birth to dying on the cross and to His Resurrection He encountered many obstacles and challenges both alone and with His disciples, but there was never a time when the road was the obstacle. Indeed, the obstacles, challenges, and tribulations encountered along the way become very important content making up the sum total of the experience along the road.

Scripture provides many examples of obstacles, trials, challenges, and tribulations become important content for the journey along the road of life and faith including the following:

Then the disciples came to Jesus privately and said, "Why could we not cast it out?" So Jesus said to them, "Because of your unbelief; for assuredly, I say to you, if you have faith as a mustard seed, you will say to this mountain, 'Move from here to there,' and it will move; and nothing will be impossible for you." (Matthew 17:19-20)

My brethren, count it all joy when you fall into various trials, knowing that the testing of your faith produces patience. But let patience have its perfect work, that you may be perfect and complete, lacking nothing. (James 1:2-4)

And not only that, but we also glory in tribulations, knowing that tribulation produces perseverance; and perseverance, character; and character, hope. Now hope does not disappoint, because the love of God has been poured out in our hearts by the Holy Spirit who was given to us. (Romans 5:3-5)

"These things I have spoken to, that in Me you may have peace. In the world you will have tribulation; but be of good cheer, I have overcome the world." (John 16:33)

A job seeker faces many obstacles, challenges, and tribulations along the road from the onset of the job search road to the final destination of full employment, but the road itself is never the obstacle even when the job seeker is convinced the road is the main problem.

As with Jesus and His disciples, the job seeker must accept the glory in tribulations, knowing tribulations faced will lead to hope and true progress along the road to full employment. The job seeker's faith may be tested many times along the job search road to full employment, but the job seeker must remain faithful to the belief even though they have only faith as a mustard seed they will be able to move the mountain of obstacles they encounter along the road.

What will help all along the journey is knowing the road is well traveled and the obstacles encountered along the road ultimately provide the things necessary to truly understand and appreciate what is to be found at the end of the job search road.

1. What obstacles have you encountered along the job search road?
2. How are you handling the obstacles as you move along the job search road?
3. Have you truly been able to eliminate the job search road as one of the obstacles you encounter?
4. What do you need to be better prepared for meeting obstacles along the job search road?

Prayer

Dear Lord, we pray we may find our way to you. Please give us the tools we need for success in our job search. Protect us and our families along our journey. Help us to reach our destination of full employment as soon as possible. Fill us with your love and keep all temptations away from us. You are the reason we have the strength to do everything we do. Thank you for the opportunities already provided for us. Through Jesus Christ our Lord, who with you and the Holy Spirit lives and reigns, one God, now and for ever. Amen.

Side With Wisdom

Wisdom, as the fashioner of all things, has been associated with God from the very being of time. Wisdom is eternal, one in being with the Father, and when personified can refer to the Messiah.

The Book of Wisdom includes the following:

For wisdom is more mobile than any motion; because of her pureness she pervades and penetrates all things. For she is a breath of the power of God, and a pure emanation of the glory of the Almighty; therefore nothing defiled gains entrance into her. For she is a reflection of eternal light, a spotless mirror of the working of God, and an image of his goodness. Although she is but one, she can do all things, and while remaining in herself, she renews all things; in every generation she passes into holy souls and makes them friends of God, and prophets; for God loves nothing so much as the person who lives with wisdom. (Wisdom 7:24-28)

Throughout history scholars have made comments regarding the nature of wisdom, and as time and technology have moved forward we even see credible comments on wisdom voiced in movies.

By three methods we may learn wisdom: First, by reflection, which is noblest; Second, by imitation, which is easiest; and third by experience, which is the bitterest. (Confucius)

Knowledge comes, but wisdom lingers. It may not be difficult to store up in the mind a vast quantity of facts within a comparatively short time, but the ability to form judgments requires the severe discipline of hard work and the tempering heat of experience and maturity. (Calvin Coolidge)

How terrible is wisdom, when it brings no profit to the wise. "Sherlock Holmes" (2009)

Nima: But great Lama, Tenzin is my brother. He works inside the tunnel, where the ships are built. But where is in your wisdom, great Lama, if Tenzin is right . . . what if our world is indeed coming to an end?

Lama Rinpoche: Like this cup, you are full of opinions and speculations. To see the light of wisdom . . . you first must empty your cup. "2012" (2009)

With time and experience a person can learn enough to display wisdom as shown by Joan Rivers when she said:

"Yesterday is history, tomorrow is a mystery, today is God's gift, that's why we call it the present."

To be completely successful with their job search the job seeker must acquire their wisdom by whatever means possible and apply their acquired wisdom to the task of getting to their next job.

1. How are you acquiring the wisdom necessary to be successful in your job search?
2. Are you having difficulty convincing others to appreciate both your knowledge and wisdom?
3. Do you sometimes have difficulty emptying your cup of opinions and speculations?
4. What would make your quest to acquire wisdom during your job search easier?

Prayer

God grant me the serenity To accept the things I cannot change; Courage to change the things I can; And wisdom to know the difference. Living one day at a time; Enjoying one moment at a time; Accepting hardships as the pathway to peace; Taking, as He did, this sinful world As it is, not as I would have it; Trusting that He will make all things right If I surrender to His Will; So that I may be reasonably happy in this life And supremely happy with Him Forever and ever in the next. Amen. (attributed to Reinhold Neibuhr, 1892-1971)

It's A Startup

Just more than two millennia ago Jesus came out of Galilee to begin His public ministry, which would become known throughout the world as Christianity. Early in His public ministry Jesus put together His initial startup team by appointing twelve apostles. Subsequently Jesus identifies an even larger group in the opening of the Sermon on the Plain, and later Jesus sends out seventy followers in pairs to prepare towns for His prospective visit.

Clearly Jesus has a plan for His public ministry, and it can be divided into three distinct stages. The first stage is Jesus' Galilean ministry, which begins when Jesus returns to Galilee from the Judaean Desert after casting out the temptation of Satan. The second stage of His public ministry is the Perean ministry, as Jesus begins travel towards Jerusalem and to the area where he was baptized, which is about a third of the way down from the Sea of Galilee along the Jordan. The final stage of His public ministry begins with Jesus' triumphal entry into Jerusalem on Palm Sunday.

The course of Jesus' public ministry includes all the parts found in any startup business plan, including perhaps the most beautifully stated value proposition the world has ever seen.

And as Moses lifted up the serpent in the wilderness, even so must the Son of Man be lifted up, that whoever believes in Him should not perish but have eternal life. For God so loved the world that He gave His only begotten Son, that whoever believes in Him should not perish but have everlasting life. For God did not send His Son into the world to condemn the world, but that the world through Him might be saved. He who believes in Him is not condemned; but he who does not believe is condemned already, because he has not believed in the name of the only begotten Son of God. (John 3:14-18)

On its own John 3:16 has been called the "Gospel in a nutshell", because it contains the most concise summary of the central theme of traditional Christianity found in the New Testament.

Job seekers are frequently told their job as a job seeker is to find their next job. In fact, the job seeker must become the head of a startup enterprise where packaging the job seeker's skills and experience coupled with a value proposition will lead the job seeker to full employment.

All employers hire only when they can either save money, make money or receive a solution for a specific problem. Thus, the job seeker's value proposition must include features, benefits, and extended benefits clearly defining their value to prospective employers in terms the prospective employers can match with one or more of the reasons why they would hire someone.

Just as any startup the job seeker's value proposition must be paired with a plan of action defining the course of their job search campaign. Failure to cover all aspects of the job search process in the job search plan will only delay the job seeker's arrival at full employment.

1. Have you actually sat down and put together a value proposition for your job search?
2. Are you having difficulty equating the needs of employers with your skills and experience?
3. What have you done to take full responsibility for your job search?
4. What do you need to complete your value proposition and job search plan?

Prayer

Lord, keep before us the wisdom and love you have revealed to us in your Son Jesus Christ. Help us to be like him in thought, word and deed. Through Jesus Christ our Lord, who with you and the Holy Spirit lives and reigns, one God, now and for ever. Amen.

Topic Index

Scripture Index

Old Testament:

New Testament:
Acts - 8, 15, 78, 98
1 Chronicles - 25, 46, 140
2 Chronicles - 70
Colossians - 57
Ephesians - 57
Galatians - 145
Hebrew - 48, 57, 62
James - 48, 65, 70, 96, 154
John - 5, 11, 232 29, 36, 54, 59, 70, 85, 94, 140, 154, 160
Luke - 1, 3, 5, 8, 21, 48, 145, 151
Mark - 11, 23, 103, 142, 147, 149
Matthew - 17, 21, 44, 54, 65, 68, 83, 92, 94, 96, 103, 106, 109, 111, 114, 117, 122, 124, 129, 132, 136, 138, 154
1 Peter - 41
Philippians - 38, 48, 120, 142
Revelation - 5, 126
Romans - 27, 70, 81, 96, 101, 111, 154
2 Thessalonians - 145
2 Timothy - 31

Secular Reference Index

About The Author

Charles Caro has been a part of the St. Paul Catholic Church "In-Between" Job Seeker Support Group (Tweeners) as a Support Team Leader since 2009. During his time with the Tweeners group Mr. Caro contributed not only his expertise with using LinkedIn but also as the author of the weekly "Reflection", which was the devotional segment of each Tweeners meeting. In addition, he is a commissioned Stephen Minister.

Mr. Caro earned a Master of Arts degree in Political Science from the University of South Florida located in Tampa, Florida. The core of his graduate studies was in the field of international business with a particular emphasis on international relations and comparative politics focusing on the oil industry and the Middle East.

He has worked internationally with software and architectural firms . His work and travel experience has taken him to many countries, including Japan, China, Singapore, United Kingdom, France, Netherlands, Saudi Arabia, Egypt, Lebanon, Bahrain, Ethiopia, Kenya, and Canada.

https://www.linkedin.com/in/carocc